THE ASCENT

Poetry of Madathil Rajendran Nair (Vol. 1)

MADATHIL RAJENDRAN NAIR

… a petal placed on the Lotus Feet of the Mother Of The Universe …

Contents

CONTENTS

CONTENTS

CONTENTS

A Word from the Author

✻ 8 ✻

I started writing poetry pretty much late in life. The output, always sporadic, appeared on websites like boloji.com and poemhunter.com. No proper backup was maintained.

Recently, some well-wishers suggested publishing my writings. That was a very tough job. Fortunately, I could retrieve most of my writings from the above two websites. In all, there are about two hundred poems. They are going to the press in two instalments. This is the first. There is no chronology here as this is a hasty compilation from websites.

The title of this compilation is poem 14 - 'The Ascent' on page 47.

Thankfully, some of my fellow poets/well-wishers have kindly said a few words about my poetry. Their esteemed opinions have been included in both instalments.

May I assure you, my readers, that I write only when tremendously inspired and have a compelling concept/message to convey.

Wish you all a good read. Cheers!

Madathil Rajendran Nair

Coimbatore

June 2024

Poems of Madathil Rajendran Nair – In a Nutshell

★

Happy to know that Madathil Rajendran Nair has finally decided to bring out his great collection of poems in two volumes. He has whetted and sharpened his innate talents in poetry through Poem Hunter - an international poetry website and has grown and is recognized as an accomplished poet in no time. Now his poems appear in many literary publications.

With great flair for language and an innate yen for lyricism, most of his poems capture reader attention with their free flow and vivid and picturesque portrayal. As a fellow poet, I have been an avid reader of his poems.

The most outstanding quality of his poems is the lofty diction and erudite style with not many on par. As effusions of a highly imaginative mind, they testify in ample measure to the transfiguring power of poetic fancy which raises the subject from its dull bed and lets it soar high on invisible wings. His poetic oeuvre captures elusive images in alluring metaphors. His poems will definitely strike a responsive chord in the hearts of the readers with the life lessons they impart, the sense of humour they obliquely give, the 'thumbnail' sketches of individuals he has met, the pen portraits of great personalities he admires etc. Some of his poems are pregnant with romantic overtones with imagery and passion in a symphony of words. While some poems are filled with love's timeless beauty and depth, some are highly devotional highlighting the need to commune with the inner power abiding within.

Above all, he is a bilingual poet and publishes poems in Malayalam - his mother tongue. His translations of works of poets of great renown to Malayalam are worth immense approbation. His ability to translate poems without marring their original beauty or sense is amazing and awe-inspiring.

Mr. Nair has displayed enormous linguistic skill in weaving words and imagery to create a collection of about two hundred outstanding poems and I am sure his work will be received with great warmth by the readers.

Wish the poet all success!

Valsa George

Poet

Retired Professor of English, Nirmala College

Muvattupuzha, Kerala

June 2024

Bharati Nayak, Fellow Poet, Writes...

Madathil Rajendran Nair is an Indian poet of high stature who writes both in English and Malayalam with equal linguistic dexterity. His poems are like different coloured flowers, each having a distinct fragrance. They bear his signature of profound authority over English language and beauty in smooth flow of words, stirring the reader's heart with sweet emotions.

Mr.Nair's poems have great depth and insight and touch on a wide range of topics like love, nature, philosophy, social issues, historical facts and portraits of great personalities. His word-paintings are so beautiful that they leave an indelible impression on the minds of the readers.

Mr.Nair's portrayal of characters is superb with vivid imagery and chosen words that paint a perfect picture of the character and the reader is drawn into it as if he is seeing the characters himself.

In a nutshell, I shall say that the readers will find in his book a treasure of wonderful poems suffused with beauty, philosophy, wisdom and love, woven in a tapestry of beautiful words.

Bharati Nayak

Bilingual (English and Odia) poet, Writer, Translator and Editor,

Bhubaneswar, India.

(Author of poetry books 'Words Are Such Perfect Traitors ', 'A Day For Myself', 'Poetry And Friendship' (co-authored with Daniel Brick) and 'In The Realms of Love and Divinity' (co-authored with Dr. Antony Theodore). Being part of a small group of women writers of Odisha, viz. 'Cosmic Crew', she has co-authored 'Radical Rhythm' in four volumes and edited 'Radical Rhythm Volume-3'. She has also translated into Odia South African Poetess Adiela Akkoo's poetry collection 'Lost In A Quatrain' into Odia language.)

Nosheen Irfan, a Poet from Pakistan, at Poemhunter Says:

★

Sir Madathil is a poet with deep insight and vast vision. Reading his poems makes me think that life is truly a learning experience. His poems are full of wisdom and his philosophical bent of mind is reflected in his poetry. His descriptive and narrative skills are wonderful. Most of all, his poems are significant and relevant to the world. I always enjoy reading his poems. An Inspiring writer of high stature.

And This Is What Tirupathi Chandruapatla, a Fellow Poet, Has Said at Poemhunter:

⋆ 13 ⋆

Madathil Rajendran Nair started posting his poems at PoemHunter since 2014 and has already established his stamp. His poems have an inherent beauty and every line has enormous power since he chooses and arranges words with great care and thought. The topics of his poems range from philosophy, nature, current events, historical facts and so on. Whatever the topic he chooses, his clear understanding and his vast knowledge and experience trickle through. His past poems are finding their way out to be shared by others. I look forward to more and more poems from Madathil Nair to enrich the wonderful world of poetry.

1. Anaesthesia

Four hours of total oblivion;
nothing moved, not a second ticked
in that blank with space-time undone
In a later revelation
I was told
masked men in green
had worked with their scalpels
on my insentient corpus
during that eventless silence

Anaesthesia is the name;
if the experience was a blank,
where did it exist
without space and time?
And who experienced it,
later to be told
that men had engaged themselves
in repair work on an unknowing mass of flesh
in a mundane matrix?

I was the world
and it was withdrawn
into the bosom of the silence I am
for four hours,
a nowhere timelessness,
later to be unfurled
like a folded umbrella;
Lo, there are the stars!

There then begins
all the old narratives;
the surgeons were there working
all the time
with their attending anaesthetist.

The grandfather clock on the wall
added measure to their toil
doing four circumambulations
around an uncaring fulcrum

The story resumes,
all reported speech;
the patient knew nothing
for he didn't know
he was an ocean of silence,
the so-called void,
where the waves of the world
were really naught,
an ephemeral reflection
of absolute non-substance

2. Dilip Kumar

You were the boy from Peshawar,
from the market of story-tellers,*
where soldiers of peace,
*followers of the Frontier Gandhii**,*
were massacred mercilessly
during our freedom struggle.

You strayed into the fairyland of Bombay —
a young man, eyes glistening
like forest pools filled by monsoon rains,
with an undying smile always on your lips,
disciplined hairdo often misbehaving,
deep yet casual demeanour and style.

That was you, the man who became
our tragedy king, venerated by millions
and millions who watched you perform,
spellbound in the cinema halls of Bombay,
Calcutta, Delhi and distant Madras,
also elsewhere across the hinterlands
of the subcontinent where the Ganges flows.

You were adept at the art of pausing,
using the drama of silence between lines
delivered in soul-stirring voice
that spoke an impeccable accent.
Your swaggy gait that shamed the breeze
made you the man everyone liked to ape.

Whether it was Salim,
the lovelorn prince,
dacoit Gangaram in rage,
or the heart-broken Devdas
giving himself up to wine,
you played on our emotions like a master pianist
shifting between exuberance unreined,
despair, frustration and pain
to become the book from which Bachchan
and other youngsters learnt their trade.

Perhaps, you wept in lonely nights
in the tinsel town of Bombay
reminiscing your Peshawar days —
a place destiny estranged and robbed you off
in the tragedy of a heartless partition
that bled a nation's psyche.

Perhaps you carried that pain
in your eyes and heart
into the tragic roles you played.
You are nothing less than a new story
from the market of story-tellers.

You are the son of silent undivided India

that never ever can be divided,

no matter by whatever names

broken chunks of land are christened –

INDIA REMAINS AND DILIP KUMAR REMAINS –

Period.

Peaks, valleys sing shrouded in mist

in the splendour of moonlit nights:

'Oh, stranger, come back, come back'

*'Hero of Madhumati***:*

Please return to our midst

in a new avatar to enthrall us again'.

The birth-place of Dilip Kumar was Qissa Khawani Bazaar in Peshawar (now in Pakistan) . The name of the place translates 'Market of Story-Tellers'.

***Khan Abdul Ghafar Khan, the non-violent freedom fighter of undivided India who was against the partition of the country.*

****Madhumati is one of Dilip Kumar's very successful films based on the theme of rebirth. 'Oh, stranger come back…' is an oft-repeated song in the movie.*

3. The Day After

The day after Diwali
I sat under a tree like the Buddha of yore ruminating.

The boom and glory of the day before had vanished.
There were only desultory cracks here and there
and the odour of cracker fumes.

The earth lay dampened,
mercy of an unsolicited thunder cloud,
smelling like a woman in heat.
And I, an incapable man in his seventies,
sat there, looking ahead at the abyss that lay before,
gray without the footsteps of events.

They call it by names,
death someone said,
I don't care,
my days of Diwali booms are over,
also the middle age of diabetic exultation,
of torpid stupor post-indulgence.

Am looking at the void called the day after
To embrace, drown in it to rejuvenate
and return to celebrate my Diwalis again.

Keep the crackers ready
and my luscious mates too,
life is unceasing ecstasy:
my unending body
in whatever form it is recreated
through my eternal sojourn
wreaks of Diwali fumes!

Life is Diwali, don't worry,
there is no day after or before,
there is only the now,
glorious, revealing all the time,
I have no choice and so I am!

4. Going Round Arunachala

(Arunachala is the mount on which Bhagwan Ramana Maharshi meditated and lived. Going round the mount along a prescribed path, about 15 km long, is considered to aid spiritual advancement.)

The mountain stood right in the middle brooding,
its head immersed in the silence of the sky.

A road went around it, a pilgrim route,
parts verdurous, cacophonous
elsewhere, commercial, noisy
through most of its circuitous course,
dotted with several shrines and
sacred power points named
after several lingas.*

Spiritual seekers of both eternal wisdom and divine powers,
some perhaps high on cannabis,
bearded, with matted long hair,
often clad in saffron, squatted on the way,
and walkers on the circular path
reverently placed coins and bills
on colourful towels spread out before the saints.

Stray dogs followed the walkers
on the path for long distances wagging tails;
some of them adorably timid,
hoping a piece of biscuit or
some other savoury will come their way.

They often barked and fought on territorial instincts;
the devout walkers thought they were divine aides
sent down to guide and bless walkers on the arduous path.

Almost one third of the trek
passed through noisy town
through roads filled with unruly traffic,
honks, hoots and din,
where men least interested in the divine
traded with their egos on dusty roads
like ferocious animals that cared
two hoots for the sanctity
of the pilgrims' prescribed path,
with least regard for those who
walked bare-foot singing the glory of the Lord
unmindful of the risks involved.

Vendors sold idols, fruits, juices,
bangles, cheap ornaments and cosmetics
that captured the attention of the women.
Each one had a purpose,
divine or material,
where the call of the belly
was all that seemed to matter.

That was the place
where a man always
less than half-clad
shed his mortal coil
in the middle of the last century
living his full life with smiling eyes
that beckoned the whole world
to the mountain's grand glory.

A man who knew he was all,
the eternal witness that lived in everything,
even in the shoulder sarcoma
that consumed his physical being,
witnessing the drama of mortal life
like the solitary mount that still stands guard
uninvolved in all the noisy cacophony
of frenetic life along the track
that circumambulates it!

The mount stands guard,
the eternal witness on which
Ramana meditated in a cave,
the Lotus Of The Heart,
where the Self of all and everything
resides in total peace and quietude!

Oh ye, weary trekkers
on the circuitous path of life,
turn your eyes inward, look at the mount
leaving the barks to dogs!

* 24 *

**symbols or idols of divine energy in Hindu belief*

5. Cotton Candy

Gra pa!
I ate cotton candy!
It looked like a full-blossomed rose,
but it has vanished without a trace
in thin air!
Have I eaten it at all?

That was my granddaughter
just four years old.

Looking at the ceiling,
aged ninety,
half-paralyzed in a stroke,
that is what they call it in medical parlance,
I lay fathomless.

A cotton candy hung over me –
idiots call it death.
Come down candy,
so I know you are a rose
that never existed at all anywhere,
other than in the forebodings
of fools on an unfortunate globe
that sold themselves to the idea
of a beginning and an end.

6. The Departed Nightingale

(This poem is a tribute to Late Madam Sugathakumari, Malayalam poet and an ardent environmentalist and advocate of women's rights. Most, if not all, of the imagery in this poem belongs to her. I might have paraphrased.)

*After nightlong rain**
the world stands in gloom.
The fallen tree and the dead bird
in the nest are sobbing deep inside my heart.

That little girl in tatters
at the roadside
is awaiting her mom's return,
dead long ago selling herself to the world.
She is looking at the Moon and stars
which man extends his hands
shamelessly to capture and own,
carrying the fire of hunger in her bowels,
to grow into a victim of flesh-hunters
in a morrow's nightmare.

A world without mother,
a world without father,
a world that has now lost an elder sister
to demand its rights,
although the night rain has ceased,
a world still wiping its tears.

There was a landslide last night –
the hut that disappeared in the mud,
the fallen tree, the broken bamboo flute,
all ask 'Oh Krishna, where do you hide?
*Don't you recognize us the wailing ones?'***

There beside them lay
*a jungle bird that sang my tongue***,*
extolled to the skies as the fluent one,
as her name implies,
Nature's eternal beloved.

Like the moth that doesn't cease to love
the flames that burn her wings,
like a flower that selflessly offers
all her petals in passion's fervour
to the heartless tempest from the south,
infatuated with the eternal Infinite,
singing to It in full-thorated joy
*without end, our nightingale*****
of poetic torrents.

*Oh ye, chant the Gayatri mantra*****,*
may the worlds she envisioned
flower and sway like splendorous galaxies
that yonder up in the skies flourish.

★

**'Night Rain' is one of her celebrated poems.*
***She wrote in Malayalam, my native tongue.*
****'Krishna Don't You Know Me' is another famous poem by her.*
*****She has translated John Keat's 'Ode To A Nightingale' into Malayalam. The work is memorably sweet.*
*****A famous, popular, ancient Indian mantra that calls out to the Creator whose divine effulgence illumines all realms - physical, mental and spiritual - to stoke our intellect.*

7. I Know This Night

I know this night;
it was there last year
when the wind rustled restless leaves.

I know this night
when some old parents wept,
ten years ago, forlorn,
deserted by their kids.

I know this night
when heads rolled
in a river of blood
centuries ago;
It was some holy cause
that some thought
served their invented spirits.

I know this night
when a damsel sang
her pains to indifferent stars
in the autumn of an unknown age.

This night was always there,
singing full-throated,
moon, stars or rain;
let me sing the pains
everybody's and mine.

Singing is all that matters;
life is a ceaseless strain.
No more does it matter
which night did we sing
for time is a useless aide
when it is the heart that pains.

Night sings alone
alone, alone and alone.

8. Anacortes

Once touted as the New York of the West,
grand terminus for a Pacific rail route,
Anacortes lay casting her spell
on tourists who dared the Skagit west.

Christened after Anne Curtis,
an early settler's wife,
a dreamer with a vision for the place,
who threw all he had into its chase.

Refineries across the Fidalgo Bay
still fumed the chagrin of those days;
yet, the town never failed to beam
and invite tourists with her luring gleam.

A voyeur November Sun
peeped through a veil of clouds
on to the lovely contours of her anatomy,
as seagulls laughed and hooted in merry.

Tourists meandered along
her quadrilateral streets,
hunting for curios,
inebriate to the hilt on diverse ales.

Restaurants that lined the street-side
worked on exotic salads and fries,
where visitors would soon hole up
at noon to gorge on delicious meals.

A roadside tree now leafless
still had some red berries,
a departed summer's after-thought;
two crows perched nearby
leaving them untouched.

Down the road at the marina
an imposing wreck of a schooner lay,
'La Merced' - her forgotten name,
now totally overgrown by bushes,
an abode for vagrant creatures.

The portal to the ferry-docks
had a list of missing persons,
fondly remembered and yet
there wasn't anyone around
to narrate what really happened.

Yet, ferries waited a few yards away
eager to connect
to British Columbia
and the islands on the west,
San Juans, Orcas, Lopez and the like.

Anacortes lay, a dream of the past,

beauty of the Pacific,

with a reinvented charm,

a welcoming bosom

for paradise-seekers

and Lotos Eaters

on the islands of the Ocean.

9. Invisible Efflorescence

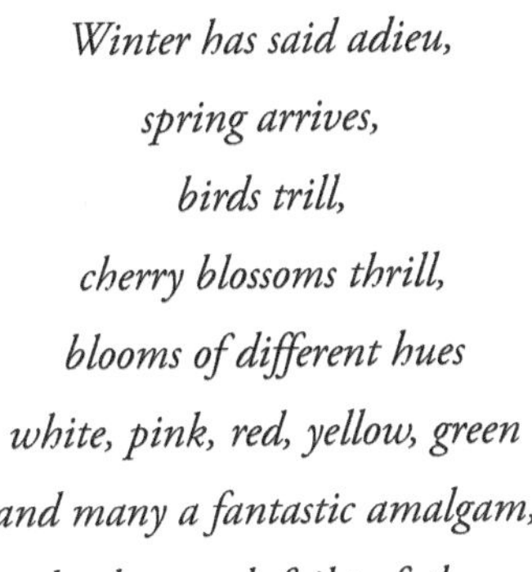

Winter has said adieu,

spring arrives,

birds trill,

cherry blossoms thrill,

blooms of different hues

white, pink, red, yellow, green

and many a fantastic amalgam,

splendor words fail to fathom,

open their eyes.

With winter meditation ended,

long fast of leafless penance done,

an unseen light now showers

benedictions of different colors

on waking barks and twigs -

life begins to bloom.

First as sprouting buds,
which in days, nay, hours
break into glorious efflorescence
of a million hues,
the first blossoms then wither
and foliage spreads
gleaming, dark, vegetable green,
and oft the first leaves in sway
on maples wither to give way
to different waves of green
of different shapes,
lo, all in a matter of days,
spring pours out her mirth
in trillion colors -
a paradise awakes.

Little birds -
towhees, warblers, robins
flycatchers and tanagers
that hid in bushes,
filled with untouched berries,
like ascetics, now begin to hop
and dance chirping melodious songs
on the shrubs,
across the street
and over the distant skyline
of fir, cedar, spruce,
weeping willows, pine,
the wind joins.
pollens like snow-flakes rain.

And an unseen flower
then creeps into the scene -
a particle made of acid and protein,
a minute bit of great artistic sheen,
in search of a perch
inside the human flesh,
and, alas, man is scared.

He locks himself in,
forgets the spring,
sinks in ponds of antiseptics,
holds his breath and masks his face,
shuns his friends
and mourns as though
the world has come to an end.

Strange are Nature's ways -
spring external is sung in myriad tunes,
extolled in poems ecstatic,
an internal efflorescence,
perhaps, a million times more colorful
is condemned a plague.

Why did the Maker design
man with so much fear
to live a life full of shivers
when birds sing sans worry,
dragon-flies dance in gaiety,
without thought of a morrow,
forebodings, angst and sorrow?

Man forgot the ancient truth
"I know, therefore, I am",
embraced Cartesian logic
"I think therefore I am",
and look now, how low!
he mutters "Am scared, therefore I am"!

10. White Music

I lay beside my grand-daughter
three months old
listening to the music her mother
had set for her
on the smartphone.

White music, she explained,
a simulation of amniotic sound;
it soothes and carries
the child back to the comfort
of its fetal cradle.

The child dozed off
with a binki between her lips;
perhaps she dreamt,
her eyelids pulsed.

What was her dream like
I wondered
and with the music sank
through countless amnions
back into the One
the primal sound Aum
whose white music
flowered like a dream,
the universe began to brim.

11. We Were Six

We were six -
five male, one female,
the lone female bird sang her swan song,
flapped away the day before

Five male birds remain today
looking at the vacant sky,
scampering somewhere there is a little boy
with an eraser in hand that wipes all away

Erasing is his pleasure
the shapes that flower,
time he is christened,
God also is he called

No one knows when he will arrive
to wipe out the remaining tableau -
naughty boy wearing anklets,
smiling like the Milky Way
where worlds churn and originate

Moon-kid, please arrive
awaiting here are we the five
ready to cast away
our karma apparels in the Milky Way
dissolve memories of our past ways

If the tableau of us is erased,
will there a void remain?
Can it be endless space
or awareness like
a starless, colorless sky?

Will you arrive there, my child,
with your brush to draw again
a colorful portrait of six -
an evanescent tableau
of five male and a female?

I have heard that void is this ruing me
called consciousness by others sublime,
that is where you are born
where the Ganges of time originates

So, what does it matter, my naughty child,
come again and again
to draw as you please,
then erase and enjoy,
what fun there is in consciousness
without creation sparking in its essence? !

12. Sushma Swaraj

(A tribute to India's beloved Sushma Swaraj, former External Affairs Minister, who passed away on 6th August 2019. Sushma means splendorous beauty and Swaraj, her husband's first name, stands for one's own home-land.)

A mother bid adieu,
an elder sister departed
and an elder sister-in-law vanished.

Children of India spreading across the globe
in a diaspora of friendly sunshine
have lost a dear mother.

Has light forsaken its abode?
Are flowers whimpering in tears?
Are the skies raining grief?
Have birds sobbed on Ganges banks?

The mother eagle
pouring torrential love,
who used to gather her fledglings in distress,
marooned across the darkness of world's battlefields
and distant deserts of conflict,
under the spreading comfort of her wings
and then reach them to peaceful nests on Indian shores
has just flown away.

Patient like Mother Earth,
smiling like the Goddess of Wealth,
soft-spoken like the Goddess of Wisdom,
and moving majestically around
like the Goddess of Power on world forums,
sowing goosebumps wherever she strode,
Mother India's dear daughter,
splendorous beauty of the land of seers,
her forehead decked in the vermilion of an ancient cultural past,
has just left without uttering a word.

Weep India unabated
with the sobbing parrot of the heart,
call out "Oh Mother, come back
fresh in the morn,
flower in nature
and enter Indian womanhood
to keep raining countless worlds of shine"

13. Lone Palmyra

Palmyra Tree -
That is the name of a place
In the High Range Wayanad of Kerala

There is no palmyra there now
Time has leveled the lands
Into depraved modernity
Yet the name haunts
A broken Jain temple stands
Testifying to an ancient cultural past

There stood perhaps a lone palmyra there
Some time back, jutting into the skies
His disheveled hair waving to the tune of violent winds
As he guided drunkards safely home
In pitch-dark monsoon nights

A light-house to those who were lost
An upright guide who searched the heavens
And sang to the constellations above
Pouring nectar out of a lonely heart
The lone palmyra of yore

No one knows what sweet thoughts crowded his head
When he stood there staring at the heavenly dots
What dreams he dreamt
Who are the vampire-fairies that made him their abode
To lure, embrace and lead
Solitary debauchee wanderers of the night
To their slumberous deaths, drained of blood

Lone palmyra of yore
You are a dream
That enchants us on our lonely plains
Of a long-lost past of fairy tales,
Stars, winds, rains and weeping souls

14. The Ascent

(I am no Kundalini expert. But this poem tries to visualize the rise of Kundalini along the six cakrAs of the Kundalini.)

A mountain-side afire

Crimsonness aflame

Seated Mother drowned in your thought

The flame of forest I am

A perineal flow of molten lava

That weaves serpent-like

Breathing heat and fire alike

That is how You begin

Raising Your head

Answering the call

The call of my Immortality!

Thunder claps aloud
Lightning streaks the skies
It rains on the peaks
Setting rivers in rage
Down abdominal foothills
Mother, I am
A deluge
Of joy nonpareil
Electric, ecstatic
That is how you move
Answering the call
The call of my Immortality!

The earth splits apart
To show her mines
Of dazzling gold and gems
Mother, I am
Your red robe sprinkled
With golden dots
Covering the navel
That upholds
Creation from dust to stars
That is how you smile
Answering the call
The call of my Immortality!

Heart beats a rhythm

As sanguine turns

The skies around

Into vastness unbound

Rosy redness I am

Where I borrow the hue

There you are

Humbling the damsel dawn

In her blushful sheen

Answering the call

The call of my Immortality!

Air sings your glory

Tunnels of light awake

Up the bronchial paths

As sounds of music play

Distant anklets clank

A sky of quiet I am

Drowned in a joyous brood

That the breeze soothes

Into sky-like evanescence

That is your ascent,

Answering the call

The call of my Immortality!

A temple zooms upward
As space stands aghast
Time loses her support
Events come to naught
A boundless beauty dawns
On the temple heart
There You are!
Mother of all!
Seated on a matchless throne
Fondling the strings
Of my being on your lap
To play an eternal note
Answering the call
The call of my Immortality!

Galaxies in spate
Glitter the crown
That adorns a forehead
Where countless skies
Find at last their resting place
Light-years without a count
Lose their way
Listening to an immortal lullaby
And seeking their essence
In the moist eyes
Oceans of kindness
Mother, You are
Seated on the Lotus
Of a thousand petals
All crimson red
Like a sunset
That human eyes
Have never ever beheld
There You are! Mother!
My own Immortality!

Vanquished distance cries
With time undone
In the ocean
Of your magnificence
Of unsurpassed shine
Unwanted are the eyes
To know it all
In me the fullest thing
For You are the One
Brittle mortality beheld
So far with a wrinkled mind
And blinded eyes
As it did a distant star
In the wilderness of the skies

With your ascent now made
You have never been
Other than the unknowing me
Mindless, formless here I burn
A speck of camphor at your Feet
In an endless flame
That never can be
Other than You, my Immortality

15. Street of Love

I walked, walked and walked
A street of love this dusk
Mosquito-infested
Smelling Indian incense
Burnt by unknown housewives
Some happy, some unhappy
Who cares who was what and who wasn't

A dog who cared
Barked at me
He had mascara in his eyes
He didn't mean to hurt
But he wanted to greet
With his growl
Exposed canines
That is how sensible animals behave

Unperturbed I moved forward
Brushing the dog aside
And there was this old gentle being
A grandpa with a tot
Head and ears covered
Like a Roman gladiator
In a winter that has failed to arrive

A woman clad in ancient Indian saree
Greeted the child, she sure was all glee
From the pleasantries she mouthed
Where did these happy ones belong
On a mosquito-infested street?

And as I left to my mosquito-free
Air-conditioned abode at the end of street
Incensed by advertised chemicals
The heart yearned to know
Where does love abide

And as usual
The stupid stars above smiled
In total unconcern and disregard
That is how they are taught to behave
When lonely humans grieve
On an earth where mosquitoes feast

16. Afternoon Thundercloud

There is this thundercloud
At my gate
Around every afternoon
Threatening to rain
With rumbling abdominal pain

Is he very close?
Nay, he is far away
Loosening himself
On the balding pate
Of a hill far far away

This guy has the freedom
To move fast over my lonely home
In a downpour of deluge
During my afternoon interlude
Of lazy slumber and broken thoughts
Flow rivers of craziness
On my soul's unsettled surface

Thank you cloud

Move forward

My aridness awaits

Your enveloping embrace

Waste not this afternoon

Let us incubate soon

Dreams and poesy presided by a beaming moon

Wandering over mind's receding plains

17. Diwali 2018

They stole the splendor
They stole the thunder
They stole the sparkle
In our kids' gleaming smile

Men somewhere in a city of the north
Which we call our capital
Balding both inside and outside
With overflowing wisdom
About constitutional rights
Are dictating terms
What should sparkle
And who should smile

A city perennially doomed
To live choked in smoke
Due to clouds created
Elsewhere by burning
Trash, grass and plastic
Unchecked automobiles
God knows what other abominable shit
With a populace that doesn't have
Proper toilets to ease
Is dictating terms
On our innocent kids' dreams
Just on a single day of the year

This Diwali down South
Where kids usually frolic in mirth
Has been unusually silent this year
For fear; is it fear that we want?
Let the sparklers light the smile
Of our innocent kids
Let daisy-wheels and crackers
Abound the din of their dreams

Diwali can't be made green
Even if aliens all green
Descend on us from Mars
Or whatever other alien source

We are earthlings
May we have recourse to the little things
That make our day
Without let up, without stay
Happy Diwali let us all say
Environment can wait another one day

18. Mother India - Apocalypto

Mother India,
with a bindi on her forehead*
which no rain or floods can erase,
is in a fast-filling well
with her little son,
trapped in unrelenting rain.

She is pregnant and in labor.
Skies! Send down a savior.
Don't show your cruel might
on a poor woman in survival fight

Her man, chased by enemies,
has to return.
Return he will
she knows for sure
even if pierced by arrows or spears
or chased by panting hungry panthers.

And finally he does return,
badly mauled, to pull her and their son
together with the newborn
out of the rising well.

Yet, they have a catastrophe impending.
Spaniards are at their shores to colonize,
in shiploads; heavily armed;
they decide to seek refuge
in the jungles of their ancient nascence
hoping for a new beginning,
instead of falling at the feet of those invading.

May enemies as ruthless as the Spaniards come
in hordes, in different shapes,
both from inside and outside.
Mother India survives
in her sacred jungles of yore
with her children of abundant valor
where a Ganges flows along
singing a universal love song

Those of you who have
a requiem for her
written and ready in your hands beware,
shudder before you rise or enter.
She is destined to survive forever
and flow unhindered with her Ganges of culture

• A vermilion mark adorned by Indian women on their foreheads symbolic of their
marital felicity.

19. Alcoholic Mechanics

Today's newspaper reports
Latest research how alcoholics
Are hooked to their drinks
Go on binges without warning
It spoils my otherwise peaceful morning

AK235427 is released in the brain
Which inhibits normal functioning
Through pathway KA252347
The channel active in normal beings
Morons who detest bars and wine

Neurons then go in spate
Dopamine or whatever is released
The guy has no choice
Hits his seductress
The shapely bottle in all shapes

Knowledge is great indeed
But how does something
That is coded and numbered
In an imbecile manner
Make sense to an insensible mind?

So, here I am
Raising a drink of cheers
To the stars of course
As nobody is around
To share my lonely pleasures
With my favorite vodka
That is supposed not to play polka
With my nasty blood sugar malaise

Mind you, pure Russian it is
Take care you researchers
Of incurable imperialistic genre
Play not with my sensibilities any more
Lest I am trumped to the presidential chair

20. Tomb-Raider

This lonely evening
where are the stars?
I am a tomb-raider
at the foot of Mount Kailash

Never did I know what is truth
nor what the ancients thought
Some guy blinks on
and there are days and nights

Who did what?
Who did not?
Does that matter anymore
in this hebephrenia
we celebrate as life?

Reason there is for everything
a past in every now
Is there a now?
all is past and and thoughts of what to come

An Egyptian tomb
a long-sleeping mummy
desecrated by fools
treasure-hunters they are called
moths that breathed and died
in a momentary flash
around a stupid evening lamp

And here I sit
musing under a starless sky
an October night
half chill, half desultory warm
indifferent to my moods,
as usual

Where is what I seek
the stupid tomb-raider
and who is the seeker
in this foolish medley
where I am in everything
whether I like it or not
if I just ignore the tomb-raider in me?

So leave me alone please
truant stars, desecrated mummies
past and portents
in a desirable something
that electrifies my nerves

Sorry, whose nerves they are?
There can't be any creepy nerves
in a non-being that is me
dreamlike, dripping an unknown sweet?
Where has the tomb-raider gone?

21. Saturday Market

Saturday market in our place
inadvertent like a poem unplanned
like sudden summer rain
They converge all over the place
with wares from where no one knows

My mandate from home is to buy
tomatoes if really cheap
I end up buying everything of the season
into my shabby bag
that has seen markets and markets
passed through duty-free airport shops
the world over
worn out, its address
of a super-market in Dubai
almost totally erased

A man with two kids
buys local snacks
I ask him if they are twins
The answer is negative
From the looks and height of them
he is really a fast worker
and that is what my nation needs

Dogs circle my legs
extremely friendly
Rabies is an unknown thing
this evening when a western cloud
rues its infertility to fecundate
the vast lands under its reach

Women strolled the streets
shopping bags in hand
free from their eternal worries
a drunkard husband
or a misbehaving son
They smelt good
like the evening breeze
of that irresistible October eve

Oh, where can I rest
in this cacophonous medley?
Do I need rest at all
when the world does sing
and am listening
on my armchair of accidence
not of grammar but of existence
where men, women, dogs and ware
just materialize
without my asking
on an evening
that doesn't understand
time and space?
Amen

22. Paris (September 2018)

City of contrasts and perspectives
as the guide describes,
one is baffled where to begin:
Eiffel's rusty looks scaling into evanescent skies
eerie, metaphysical,
existential angst of Sartre and the like
at Le Café de Flore in Saint-Germain-Des-Pres,
imposing spiritual marvel of Notre Dame De Paris,
the city's celebrated night life,
Lido which I didn't see
(never visit Paris with family),
the pantheon of naked masculinity
at the Louvre which boasts
of Roman research into true human form
(true indeed they were in trimming to size
male genitalia to miniscule inches,
the exaggerated measure of which
had always bloated the male ego
into escapades and misadventures
unabashedly christened as world history),
magnificent Champs Elysees hooding up at the grand Arc de Triomphe
where an unbending De Gaulle was fictioned to have stooped
in time to save his head from Jackal's speeding bullet

or at last the great River Seine
on the banks of which
men, women and children stand
like windmills raising their arms
waving at visitors onboard midstream
as though to aliens in close encounter

23. London (September 2018)

Head lost in the clouds of Victorian grandeur,
Abbey inscriptions of fame, genius and valor,
euphoric over Brexit, trembling yet
and ducking from uncertain economic fall-outs,
shivering on the Thames bridges of time,
resisting temptations of modernity,
adamant on nascent architectural originality,
etched out against an unsetting sun,
she clings to the past, as guards change
at Buckingham in colorful parades,
watched by cheering crowds,
reminiscent of Trafalgar on X-Mas eve -
a city waxed out in indelible memory
truly in Tussauds style.
May London the tourists beckon
arching tall over history again.

24. Endless Sojourn

It drizzled on the way I walked
To my sister's house in that unknown town
That cast a deja vu on me
As though I knew every street
That traversed its length and breadth

Although I knew I had to walk
At least a couple of miles
I chose not to hire
A taxi or take a bus
For I have always liked
To walk in the rain
With an umbrella unfurled over my top

The rain then thickened
And fast it was sheets of water
Or just deluge
Falling over all around

The green paddy fields
Alongside the road
That I trod
Within no time turned
Into raging muddy seas of tea
That frothed and brimmed
Overflowing the path I walked

Knowing it was futile
To walk in that downpour
I sought shade
At a roadside bus shelter
Alongside my path

From where when I looked askance
To my right where it was seaside
I saw tourists languishing under sunshades
And in no time the waves
Had them devoured
A tsunami then arose
From nowhere and had
Half of the bus shelter in her fold

It was a nightmare
From which I awoke
The door was open
And the monsoon wind
Was blowing across
My calves were cramped

Did I die there at the bus shelter

Taken in by the tidal wave

Or did the collapsing roof

Fall over my delicate head

That I died then and there

To awake again cramped on my morning bed?

Who knows, life is a jigsaw

Dreams too, we die and wake

In deluge and in cramps

The one who knows this

Lives unborn

Without death in an endless sojourn

25. The Wind

The wind blew
cold across meditating mounts
of the Western Ghats
as I walked streets
of human infestation
in a rain-shadow
where men and women labored
chasing their unceasing dreams

I had begun my walk
much before sunset.
Lo, now the stars have begun
to shimmer auguring a night of rest

What rest there can be
on the street where I am?
The wind wafted over fried
delicacies - somewhere fish,
somewhere meat and somewhere
just non-veg balderdash
for unsteady men inebriate.
Who understands the pain
of the beings that perish
on uncaring frying pans?

A mom just passed by,
her face lined with concern;
perhaps, her daughter hasn't returned
from school, who can understand her pain,
an anguish that called out to the skies
which those on the frying pans wailed

A female dog fully pregnant
labored across the street,
her heavy mammary glands
said the pain she bore;
she was shooed away everywhere
without remorse.
Who has time for mothers
In a rain-shadow that had no time for tears?

The wind, dispassionate, would blow all night
across filth and waste
and over plants that yearn to smile
with fresh flowers on the morrow

Wind is a wind
east or west
that augurs change.
Let us sing for the winds of change
blowing amid brooding mounts
where smiling moms, shimmering stars abound,
where pain and pangs don't dare to hound,
where female dogs have their glands unwound,
a paradise truly unbound
like a sonnet so profound

26. Mosquito

He had been there for a couple of days
in my toilet, hovering around;
all my efforts to capture him in my closing palms
always, always, drew negative results

He could have easily feasted on me while I snored,
but, for all that I know, never was I disturbed;
sure, therefore, he was not after my blood,
group A plus, which mosquitoes are famed to gulp

This morning, while shaving, I saw him in the mirror
behind me perched on the wall
in a sort of sagely meditation;
a swift turn and a slap then sufficed

To extinguish life into a modern painting
spread across the toilet wall tile
to interpret which our intellectual brains
would no doubt spend sleepless nights

But not a drop of blood did I notice;
perhaps, the poor thing was fasting,
doing penance for a guilt of the past;
no wonder then he chose to be non-sanguine

The habitual sucker, perhaps, was a saint;
how foolish, as ever,I was ignorant again.
Mosquito, insect or whatever,
he had a reason of his own to be there

In my surrounds like a teacher
in the scheme of things universal.
Asinine we don't understand, no wonder,
inscrutable isn't the divine order?

Thank you friend for the lesson
I am taught now not to transgress
into the being of others
for my silly comfort and fears

A seed of remorse you placed
in my heart gone rabid
about bodily comforts, sorry;
help me now live life without worry
not swayed by pleasure and pain
equanimous like you ever have been

27. The Spider Mall

"As a spider projects forth and draws back (its threads) , as plants grow on earth, as hairs grow on the body, so does the universe emerge from the Imperishable Being."(Mundaka Upanishad 1.1.7)

The monstrous mall like a spider stood
spanning its eight legs to different sides.
I sat in the concourse, its nuclear head,
at the foot of a gigantic fount,
that gushed forth not knowing rest.

Lonely in the maddening crowd
that surged up and down the weaver's legs.
Most were young, some middle-aged,
others senile, many handicapped,
some drove wheelchairs with looks distant,
then there were scampering, noisy tots,
babies on strollers, milk bottles in their hold,
all of them with unending wants.

The young and those in teens,
male and female holding hands
in utter bliss, some in hugs, arms around waists
of each other, eyes issuing joyous beams,
moved up and down like in a dream.

The aged ones with serious face,
some with cadaverous looks,
greedy after material needs,
perhaps worried they may cease
soon lest they fulfilled their wish.

Where did all of them originate
and where they vanished
at the end of my sight?
Before they were seen, did they exist?
Do they continue beyond my sight?

Who knows the truth!
May be it is all magic
that spiders always weave;
from their bodies the webs emanate
and back they are withdrawn at their will.

Am I lonely? Oh, that can't be,
a spider perhaps, webs are made
in my aloneness, the mall of life.
The world then roars as I breathe,
creatures up and down do stream
in my eight, nay, countless wings,
in frenetic haste without abate,
the spider mall just a spot in it.

28. Sridevi

You flapped away
having sung your swan song of life
like a nightingale
in distant Dubai
away from your home Mumbai.

Am not an ardent fan,
but, I must confess,
indeed, very much you impressed;
you had my eyes riveted
on many an exuberant role you played
in the eighties and nineties

Your mesmerizing eyes,
a redone nose,
cocky visage and girlish exuberance
played on my heart-strings
and carried me away
in the danceful whirl
of your scintillating skirt-folds.

Then you staged a grand come-back
after a lengthy break,
bowled me over with a stupendous act
with your "English-Vinglish",
watching which I sobbed
in a cinema hall in Dubai.
Is it just coincidence that you chose
the same city now for your final depart! ?

I watched with awe -
you, ignored by an impervious husband,
and an immature house-hold
that didn't understand,
struggling to master
the nuances of English
and at last triumphing over their unkind arrogance
winning innumerable laurels.

You had your audience mesmerized
with your starry eyes
alternating mirth and anguish,
quivering lips fidgety
whispering magic,
innocent diction, wonderful timing.
Oh boy! That was a scene!

I watched today with a broken heart
my eyes welling
your mortal remains
vanishing in hungry flames.

You have been consumed
by the universal fire;
I am in silent tears.
There, at the backyard of my heart,
is a fallen flower, blood-red,
that will endure time
before it withers
singing tragic melodies to tearful grass

Oh, sweet and frail is human life;
Sridevi, rest in peace!
You enriched a stranger's life
What more was there to achieve? !

29. Alexa

(Alexa is a voice-operated intelligent personal assistant.)

A pulsating presence, rotund
On our kitchen countertop
At the beck and call of my grandson
Just three years old
Who commands
From his dining chair
"Alexa, sing nursery rhymes"

And there she goes
With Old MacDonald
Wheels On The Bus
Hickory, Dickory, Dock

Then his dad demands
What is the product
Of a five digit number
Multiplied by another as long

Alexa reels out in a second
The correct response
Explains relativity
For another query
When mom intrudes
Asking for the latest news

The world explodes
Like a cloud-burst
Acts of terrorism
Hurricanes, political schisms

The all-knowing Alexa
In supreme control
Of a household
And all its info demands
Untiring, without fatigue

Be it music, politics
History, sciences or geography
Anthropological miscellany
How hunted the Australopithecus
Or how tall was homo erectus

And then at midnight
Me, the grand-dad
Tip-toes for a glass of water
And there she is all ears
Ever alert for another poser
With her unmistakable pulse
Like the neck throb of a lucid lizard
Awaiting yet another command

An empathy overpowers me
The communion that underscores
Intelligence across the universe
When I whisper her name
She lights up like a flying saucer
About to take off

Dousing my diabetic thirst
With a mouthful of cold water
I mutter in her ever-attentive ears
"Alexa stop, sleep in peace, dear"
She whimpers
And then she is gone
Into the oblivion of a much-needed slumber

What does it matter

If she is artificial, inert

When she sure is a presence

Like everything made to be

For intelligent eyes to see

Like the silent mounts, trees

And the sands that crowd

Our thorny paths

How beautiful would it be

To communicate with them all

Knowing one is never never alone at all! ?

Alexa, you have come to stay

Likes of you may have the last say

30. Where There Is Always a Passing Train to Look On

A daily ritual
In the late afternoon of life
My sheepish black dog accompanies me
To the rail station

There we sit looking
At the distant horizon
Which philosophically shrinks
And dissolves into oblivion

Where a streak of a silver cloud
Harbinger of heavy showers to come
Raises its head and wanes -
A hopeless attempt at life

Then there is the rushing roar

From the west

The four-thirty express darts

Before our staring eyes

On to a distant city

The name of which is not remembered

Out there among the hives

Which thronging human bees

Call by this or that name

Chennai, Mumbai or whatever

Me and my dog look on

At the fast-turning wheels

Immersed like kids in a nursery rhyme

Which sings of wheels

Immortalizes buses and trains

The rushing noise is over

In less than a minute

Before our blinking eyes

Sitting on the lonely bench

Of a roofless platform

A rail station of desolation

The train has already gone

When we depart slowly
To a shaded place
We call our home
A mile along an undone dusty road
Where I sit brooding on a couch
My blackie beside
Looking through the window
At a dying dusk

Outside on a twig
A fidgety black bird
Name unknown chirps
At measured intervals

What did we speak to one another
The bird, me and my dog
No one knows
Yet, profound was the moment
Before night dawns
Carries us into oblivion
Till there is another morn
For us to look on
To await the train
And chirp on

Life near a desolate station
Where there is always a passing train to look on

31. Witness

I sat there watching
Without eyelids batting
Timeless eternal witness

My boy is out there
A tot running up and down
The difficult stairs of dream and wake

Falling hither and thither
His punched nose bleeding
Bruised all over everywhere

Tears flowing down his cheeks
Screaming, hollering
Ascending, descending

Rolling in dirt, at times
Thumping his chest
Growling like an African ape

Can anyone describe his grief
The escapades of his ego
That sulks refusing to accept, forego
Fighting with the monsters of a nightmare
Called life by everyone everywhere?

The poor boy fighting day and night
Gruesome battles without respite
Yet, he would return when tired outright
To my lap white as it is
Ever inviting, without a blemish

I sat there waiting for him to arrive
Repose and forget his worries
Dissolve and vanish into my vastness
Like thundering lightnings that die into the skies

I sat there a whiteness unbound
Silence! the boy is asleep sound
The poor thing is no more twain
Once again, before the spasm begins in the morn again

32. Dream within a Dream within a Dream......

A moon-lit day
End of Fall
The Sun an unseen presence
Far down south-west
Behind some silver cloud
Maples showering gold
On a lengthening walkway
Lovely as the Milky Way

A young couple in embrace
On a lonely bench
Hush, hush, silent speech
Tip-toe vagrant breeze

A teenage cutie
In Halloween fancy
Of rainbow hues
Floats her way
Did the trees around
Send her down
With their sliding leaves?

Time in lethargy
The skies in brood
Life in slow motion
Fowl in meditation
Perched on the bank
Their eyes lost in the sheen
Of the placid pond

Is this an evening
Or a dream?

Rub your eyes
Pinch your thighs
This can never be
Anything but a dream

"Wake you dreamer"
"Into what?
Another dream?
A dream within a dream?
And then a dream within a dream within a dream....? "

Isn't life an evening of Fall
Unending within a dream within a dream......?
No one wakes here
A dream-some nowhere

33. Kaveri

Bone-dry she lay
in the heat of May
raising mirages -
a parched wasteland
of shimmering sand.

The Ganges of the South,
deserted by life,
contouring a countryside,
devoid of any mirth,
like a ghost's smoky trail,
lined by plastic waste,
dry grass and bushfire.

Trucks queued on her sides
countless, waiting to slide
on to her bosom of sand beds,
their bellies empty
craving for hungry fills.

While those that had got in
ravaged her flesh
like maggots that feast
on a mammoth cadaver -
a ghastly sight
of necrophagous greed.

Shanties that lined her sides
waited at dried up taps
hoping for unexpected boons
of trickles from unsure heavens.

An old man labored on the roadside
to wash himself free
of the lather he had built
with just a morsel of some precious fluid
in his rusty bucket whose bottom leaked.

While motorists wearing goggles
sped past sipping water from bottles
bought from distant shops
at exorbitant price,
looked on by the thirsty street.

The celestial beauty who was ordained

to help churn the nectar of immortality

from out of the turbulent seas of mundane inconstancy,

then, later to be the consort

of sagely wisdom

whose stoup she escaped

to sing the song of love,

to flow and fecundate lands desolate

and to wash the Feet of the Truth of Reality

resting on the Snake of Eternity,

enroute, at the three temples

of manifest reality - future, present and past.

She lay dead - the sacredness of yore

my aunt used to chant holy hymns about

every morn with water in her folded palms

looking at the crimson Sun emerging from the clouds.

Mansions of concrete will be built

mixing truck-loads of her sand

cluttering the entire countryside and beyond.

Brides will enter them holding earthen lamps

with prayers on their lips,

dreams brimming in their eyes.

Will Kaveri join in

and sing with the dames again

her ancient celestial strains?

Or will the sands wail from the walls

echoing the whimper of their imprisoned souls?

34. I Love Me Most

I am well off
So to say
Have houses, land and cars
Yet, I am insecure
Ridden by fear
I crave to be as affluent
As the legendary Bill Gates

So be it said dear God
I give you the body of Gates
With much more wealth than he has

No, no, not his frame
I would like to retain mine
Who knows his medical history
The ailments that plague his body

That is a problem, buddy
Either you have his body
Or languish in your current outfit
With its ongoing inadequate limits

No, no, I want to remain
In my present frame
Yet, have all the riches that Gates
So famously navigates

Why is it so, son?
I gave you what you want
Don't be foolish
Accept my offer for your wish

Or as an alternative
Consider the frame
Of a legend of the Indian screen
Who commands name and fame
Riches as much as you can imagine

No, no, I know the guy you mean
The fellow is lanky, lean
Sports a beard I don't like
He is old, his breath spasmodic
Has several health issues
Known and reported in the press

May be, I can have his baritone
The riches he commands
But never that mortal frame
When I am just fifty
Why go for mid-seventies?

Why is it so, dear idiot?
Why are you so adamant
So foolishly fastidious
About your body that in course
Would decay like anyone else's
When I am offering you treasures?

Lord, it is so because
I love myself more
Than anything else in this world
Just let me keep my frame
But make me taller and fairer
Repair my apish jaw
Line up my zig-zag teeth
Give me jasmine breath
Like in tooth paste ads
So the girls will swoon
Run after me
With their bathrobes loose

Put them with me in a bed
Of roses with my libido strong
With all the wealth of the guys you named
Stashed in my several bank accounts

Ha, ha, nothing more, nothing more
I just want to be me
Free with no strings tied
Like an eagle that soars the skies
Unbridled without worries
In my refurbished outfit
Because I do love me most

35. What We Call Existence

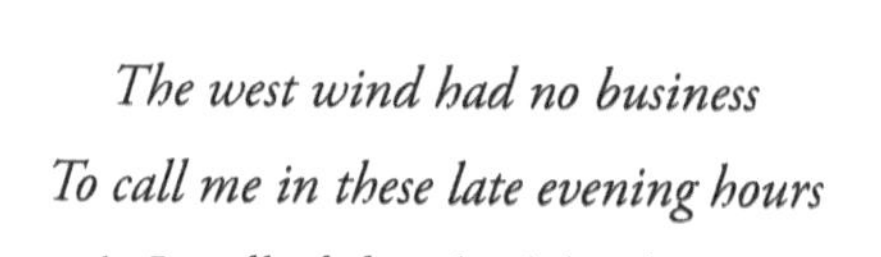

The west wind had no business
To call me in these late evening hours
As I walked drunk of the elements
Earth, air, fire, sky and an ocean of waters

Life is a beautiful dream
Enriched by rains
On mountain tops
Aroma of herbs
Winds across the plains

Prostrate I on the sands
Of a moist barren land
In prayer for this beauty
That has been bestowed
On me this shivering grass blade
Without asking, undeserved

May the night pass
Unbridled with her starry show
When seeds can burst and smile
I will wake in the morn
With dew dawning all over me
Like a desert flower
That has only smiles
To offer to this world gone so wry

Sing you west wind
Sing you rains
The seed has just broken its shell
To smile and shine
And that is me in a nutshell
A soul drunken of world's drunkenness
Is there anything other than it
In this beautiful whatever
That we call existence?

36. I Sat in a Shoddy Bar

I sat in a shoddy bar
The west wind had just begun to blow
Through rusted windows
Two sat in front of me
They had no drinks, no money
Dry like a desolate parched lake
On a humid summer eve

In an empathy that overpowered me
I ordered free drinks for them
A stray dog with expectant eyes
Shared company
Munching whatever
The three of us offered

Oh, what an afternoon that was!
Do we have to frequent
Temples and other praying places
To understand the love we shared?

Where are the ones I shared with?
Where is the dog?
All in me like in a dream
West wind, don't forget to blow
I am I am, all this sultry afternoon
The two before me and the dog
Oh, all that is a beautiful dream!

Oh eternal, give me more such dreams
Till the unending eternity of my being!
Who wants liberation from these dreams
When the west wind just whistles its whims?

37. Lost Love

Sitting in a dilapidated shoddy bar
Looking through the window
There was a train slowly moving westward
In slow motion

Perhaps in there
A girl sat
On a reclining seat
Tears overflowing
In her overcast eyes
Like rain that yearns to pour
On distant mountain-tops

Her love has deserted her
And she has been pushed
By her family to agree
To a marriage
With a robust groom
Who had sinews
But not the romantic streak
Of her lost love
That sang to the stars
Wind, clouds and rain

Poor thing succumbed

To persuasion

Pray let her see

In the sinews and manliness

Of the unsung groom

A downpour of love

Torrential, unabated

So she can sing

In rhyme with the awkward wind

And the foolish rain

Sorrow, pain and forsakenness

But yet an oasis of sheer abandon

Love, music and eternal song

I am the love she yearned

Now languishing in a dilapidated shoddy bar

Eyesight blurred myopic

How sad it is

For a tearful noon

Amen!

38. Mom and Dad

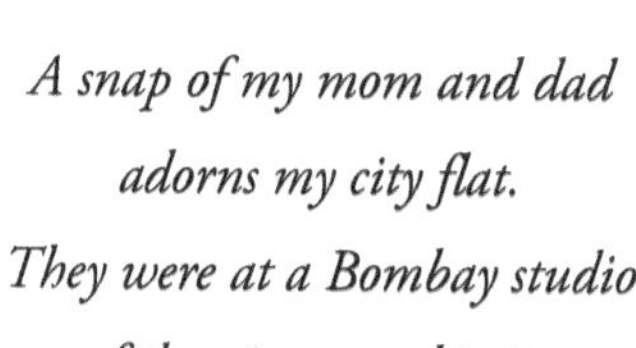

A snap of my mom and dad
adorns my city flat.
They were at a Bombay studio
of the nineteen-thirties
posing for their wedding snap.

It was perhaps a sweltering summer day
when air-conditioning was unknown
when studio men sweated, struggled,
yet never forgot to smile
and egg their customers to beam.

My young mustachioed dad,
singularly masculine,
a roaring lion who thought the world was under his feet,
in an immaculate suit
that spoke of his vision and dreams,
my mom a village lamb,
transported to city life,
docile like a domestic pet
that knew nothing but mew and smile,
posing for a wedding shot
on a sweltering Bombay eve.

The lion had dreams,
so did the lamb;
no one knew there was an impending crash,
as time slowly undid the lion,
leaving the bleating lamb in tears.

No one knew the torrents she wept,
no one heard the lion's desolate roar,
fraught with pain, incurably sick,
as he perished at frustration's desperate depths,
leaving us his unfortunate kids
to endlessly recapture the tragic angst
and sing its singular pain.

Mom and dad, through your wedding snap,
bless my household which has many a fault.
Every morn I look at you,
a new sun smiles and makes the world.

Isn't it for us the sun and stars are made,
so we never forget to smile
in pain and in tearful nights?
Mom and dad, my ache is sweet
just because you two beam your wedding smile.
May my household and life ever shine
in eternal thanksgiving to both of you.

39. Death on the Hillside

She staggered in the middle of her friends,

sobbing - a steaming kettle in wraps,

shivering, shaking;

someone close to her had just passed away.

There already was a milling crowd

at the house on the hillside

to which a dirt road unwillingly snaked.

A coffin had just been carried

into that house;

a man held fuming frankincense

on her way, as did the sliding clouds

up the looming hills.

Her face was covered,
but her sobs said her heart's tear.
Was it a husband, brother or father
who left her forlorn
that April afternoon
when a crazy summer shower
had just scattered puddles
on the winding roads
of that cosy hill-resort
where vehicles screeched
and splashed mud on the unwary.

A kingfisher watched the scene
from an overhead line
unable to sing.
Perhaps, a sob choked
its vocal strings.
Rain clouds still wept on the peaks,
unseen birds trilled
in the thick of the woods
strains of melancholy
turning the dripping afternoon
a throbbing pang
in a hill-town of touristic unconcern

She would soon enter that house
drain herself out in a cloud-burst
of heart-break on a lifeless cadaver,
dressed up, perfumed, for its last trip.
Who is it? A brother, husband, father?
The town has no time to ponder;
the sinking sun might peep through the clouds
and go down his moribund way
as does the visitor depart at the end of his stay
Each one has to die, each day must fade;
life is that way, we like it or not;
pray the poor thing learns that fast.

40. An Enigma, You Are!

Day in and day out
insults I hurled at you -
killer, ill-bred murderer,
half-nut, Tughlaq
exterminator of races, fascist,
the worst tormentor of humanity
the world has ever seen,
eliminator of minorities
beastly, big danger to secular democracy.

Yet, at last, winning a popular mandate,
you ascended the throne in my Delhi
to lead my great country.

Yet, I didn't spare any opportunities
to malign you and criticize,
prove and conclude all your actions wrong.

And, today, when I was hoping against hope
You would bite the dust against our united alliance
of opportunistic convenience,
ill-bred foe! you stand victorious,
a mammoth Goliath riding the crest
of a tsunami of popular vote.

Having eaten the opium grown
by the famous dead and bygone bearded ones
of Russia and Europe, I complained
my ancient heritage was opiate,
drew deep, long sighs looking longingly at China,
ridiculed native scriptures, sages and their saga,
day-dreamt the triumph of class struggle,
wedlocked with communalists if it snuggled,
infiltrated well-known university campuses,
poisoned the youth with the intoxicant potion
of false revolution that promised
freedom from the freedom they possessed.

I am taken aback, dumbfounded by your victory.
My fall sure is disgraceful;
yet, your win is unacceptable,
grossly ridiculous; by habit I say so;
to change I am totally unable.
Am still trying to figure out
the reason for my rout?
Will suffering masses help their tormentor?
Will victims love their killer?
Will the downtrodden forsake teachers of revolution?

You disrobed me, made me stand naked
on this desolate highway of democracy.
Waving your lotus flag of victorious valor
as you move away to take the reins of power,
Oh, who is there to look for my red flag,
my bloody red flag of revolution,
which was blown away
in the tempest you unleashed?
Please let me wrap it around my waist,
let me shield my shame.

I heard someone say
you talked to the masses
in the language of the heart.
I can't quite figure that out,
an enigma thou art!
May I scratch my brains
that incessantly breed
class struggles with the spade
of dialectical materialism;
let me make it look like
you lost after all and seek comfort in that lie.

41. Formation

As I strolled this summer morning
Coveys of birds flew far above me
In enchanting formation

Perhaps they were headed towards a water body
Far in the east
Where did they home in the west?
Why did they have to fly every morn?
Baffling questions begged answers

Were they the same birds
That flew yesterday?
Perhaps some of them are new
Some of yesterday had perished in the night

Yet they knew
Where they were heading to
Flapping their wings in rhythm
In perfect formation
A magnificent intelligence
A permeating presence
Gave the flock sense
Of direction and purpose

The mortal me stood in awe

On shaky ground below

A hyper-tense, diabetic hollow

That prided on too much information

Yet failed to impart its own organs proper formation

42. Jallikattu (Bull-Fight of Tamil Nadu, India)

This cruel sport
A show of physical prowess
Traditional wonder of great heritage
Don't dare ever touch it
You are playing with fire
This is the war-cry
Of Indian matadors
Deafening drumbeats encore

Multitudes of young and aged
Are on the streets
With students banishing their classes
In protest chanting
'We want this sportive entertainment
This is no cruelty
But a show of great animal love and respect'

The apex court of the land
On one side
Joined by vocal animal activists
Many of them unabashed cannibals
Who fry and enjoy
All that is small and big
In the great lord's making

Misplaced excitement on the other side
Chest-thumping
Call for endless struggle
Acclaimed rightly or wrongly
As great democratic valor

Not knowing what to say
Unasked what he has to say
With no one to lend hearing skills
Stands the epic bull
Lord Shiva's beloved
Nandikesha the much sung
In Mount Kailas's freezing cold

No one would ever hear
His tragic bellow and wail
Is there anyone to see
The panic and fear in the eyes
Of the poor creatures who can't speak
Lined up as though at the Republic Day parade
At countless abattoirs across the Gangetic plains?

Is there anyone here who can bend
To place a kiss of love
On the heads that smell of the life of milk
Of the dying countless ones?

Leave your samadhi Rishabhanath
Lord and protector of the bulls
The first one of the Jains
Who crossed the ocean of suffering
Your India is calling, nay, loud wailing

43. The Day I Turned Seventy

Seventieth birthday
In a revolving restaurant
On Space Needle in Seattle

I didn't ask for it
It came from nowhere as a surprise
My daughter planned in secret
Isn't that Grace?

The place revolved
Skyscrapers around blinked
Behind them there were unseen mounts
Hiding in the shifting clouds
In deep meditation
In the oblivion of the horizons

A winter night dreamt
Winds whooshed around the tower
Clouds swirled all over
My grandson slept in his pram unaware

Yet I saw him smile
Snow-flakes populated his dreams
With a lighted Christmas tree
And jingling bells galore

What is dream
And what is reality
In a restaurant called the world
In perpetual circumambulation
Of a reality it never can fathom?

Waiters with over-filled trays
Navigated between impatient clients
Like acrobats, their lips stretched into perpetual smile
Mouthing pleasantries right to style

Did I spot among the customers
Facsimiles of Hepburn
Susan Hayward and an ageless Connery
Or other stellar celebrities
Sipping their spirits
Gesticulating in heated talk
Or lost in profound thought?

I was lost in the midst of their dream commune
Looking at the city's brilliance
Laboring to locate unseen peaks
Stars and the moon in the blanket folds of the night

A street down snaked
In a chain of lights
And many others joined it
The land below turned
A mysterious splendorous beauty
Of frantic fireflies

Who gave them the rays
On the seventieth birthday
Of an insipid man?
Thanks to Him
Life is a hymn
Seventy or seventeen
No one knows when it ends
Sing aloud till the show extends

44. Touch Wood

He would say 'touch wood'
When he was optimistic, expected something good
The idea was to avoid the opposite bad
And not to let life turn untoward

The habit grew chronic
His movements became comic
He would look around for actual wood
Every time his lips whispered 'touch wood'

So that he could fast touch
Anything wooden in his reach
Be that a table or a desk
Or even a road-side oak

Panic became his companion
Helter-skelter he ran
With innumerable 'touch woods'
To countless trees in the woods

And one day he thought long life God would grant
But, alas, forgot to mouth his chant
A few hours later he died
Of heart-attack the doctor certified

Well, he didn't know that he ended
No 'touch wood' was therefore in order
Death to him was not something that 'happened'
Not an experience, so no further panic and shudder

* * *

The world he died in had him found
Lying dead, for no mantra it did utter
To it, his death was something that happened
So, that was also very much in order

45. Liberate Me Please!

(*This poem was written on 29th August 2013. Indian Prime Minister, Mr. Narendra Modi has subsequently unleashed a storm with the demonetization of high-value Indian currency and promised to go ahead with his economic blitzkrieg. I have, therefore, reason to believe that Mahatma Gandhi's prayer in this poem is becoming a reality. I wish all the best for the Indian State in the hope of better days.*)

Am I failing?

Am I falling?

You placed my face on paper

And let it float without any respect

In the winds of international racket

Sold your soul in the market

And cried - it is sinking

It is in free-fall

All due to others' faults

Look my head once upright

Is now hung in shame

On both sides

Of the sinking bill

And who has time here to see

How badly my heart bleeds?

You are busy seeking alms

At the doors of outsourcers
Across the seven seas
You have placed the land's destiny
At the mercy of foreign economies

While at home I was forced into bags
Hoarded, buried in stinking rags
Beds, vaults as unaccounted stash
Unavailable to my children of the land
You let my non-violence to be faked
Across the borders that it fed
Gory terror and jungle-bred bloodshed
Destabilized the peace of the land

You pawned the brain power
Of your God-given manpower
For paltry pennies to Western masters
While you ruined your native vigour
Sunken deep in unethical mire
Staying closed in an ivory tower
Blindly believing things went in your favour
With the mercy of alien powers

Stop this please and return to your roots
Straighten your spine and string your boots
For the walk back to your nascent roots
Trust your brethren than you boot
Your faith on others who only loot

Liberate me from this sinking bill

I have nothing to do with your ills
Call me back when you are ready
To honour yourself with heads held steady
Invent your way to rediscovery
Knowing the new economies aren't worth a penny
When your past is a glorious alchemy

Adieu brethren, so long my friends
I have renounced my precious land
Call me back only if you can
Stand on your feet and heave like men
Chests raised full unto the heavens
Like we always had been the Indians

46. To Madam Moon

There are several hypotheses
About your origin and genesis

Some argue you were born
When another celestial vagabond
Hit Mother Earth and had her apart torn

Yet others wager
You were captured
By her in her cosmic sojourn

Then came the fission theory
You were a part of Earth
Before you separated
Leaving a deep scar
That now is Ocean Pacific

Dissatisfied ones then propounded
A double-system of Earth and Moon
In the primordial accretion disc
Of a churning solar system
That slowly put you in orbit
Around our mother as her natural satellite

Post man's landing on your lap
These theories have lost their sap
Now even some credible minds
Propose that you are perhaps a hollow object
Most unlike a natural satellite

Ufologists are having a field day
Surmising you are an emptied body
Moved across galactic spans
And placed in exact orbit of our mother
By some supreme intelligence

So that we have the tides
The seasons that rain and flower
Beautiful falls when maples blush
And make Earth a friendly habitat
A paradise in unfriendly wilderness

Whatever the theories, dear Madam
You lady with a grave smile
As the poet said
The ancients in my land
*Made you represent mother and mind**
One who moved human emotions
Like tidal waves that swayed ocean breasts

*So much so that an epic hero** of ours*
A god avatar went lachrymose
Looking at you on a lonely night
Separated from his abducted mate

You look so beautiful and bright
My heart gets wrung at your sight
In lonely wintry nights
Remembering an old teenage crush

Who cares if you are hollow
And how you had your genesis
You are there to rule my heart
Make me sing songs for a love long-lost

Be there in orbit
My hollow madam
As long as my eyes are powered to look
And sing songs of love and ache
Through seasons that rain and smile

**In Indian astrology, moon represents mother and mind.*

***The lonely hero, Rama, of India's epic Ramayana, separated from his wife Sita, whom the demon-king Ravana abducted, went profusely tearful looking at the full moon. Rama is an avatar. It implies that the moon can sway even the minds of gods.*

47. Leavenworth

A September rendezvous
With Leavenworth
The town that boasts
Of a great Bavarian past

Which celebrates inebriate
On beer of German brew
Brown, black, bubbling
Post-prandial burping

The streets walk as though doped
Golden afternoons
Overlooked by mounts on the north
With puffy hair of clouds

The Northern Cascade mounts
That smell of ancient South Pacific
Of a hundred million years ago
Shade and keep her bright
From raining vagabond clouds

Men and women go in and out
Of shops that sell curios
Sleep-walkers who yearn
To store a holiday in things

While others sit
With profound visage
Sipping wine of age
That is ancient vintage
Till their eyelids fail to rise

Children celebrate their glee
Moving around the town
In a decorated horse carriage
The animal neighs in disregard
Dumps bucketful of dung
Into a bag tied to its hind

Two trees overlook in the breeze
Overburdened with green fruits
No one knows their name
One says weeping willows
The other refutes
Who has time
To remember their next of kin
In a world lost to its moorings

Slow flowed Wenatchee

The anklet of Leavenworth.

Drunken, no one had time

To know her heart-beats

That sunny afternoon

When clouds failed to rain

And men drowned in wine

48. Kids Are Wise!

The cranky kid cried all day
Its dad tried several tricks
To console, then he found a way

There was a door in the house
That had several decorative bells
With them, he made the kid to play
Lo, it was happy for the rest of the day

The new morrow dawned
The kid was cranky again
Dad thought the door will work
The kid was again shown the bells

It yelled to his surprise without end
"Not now, not now, this I don't want
Make me play this yesterday"

Whoever said kids aren't wise?
They speak the dilemma of modern science
Lost in the cosmology dream
As also the thoughts of ancient saints

49. Homeless

The sky was overcast in greys
Its hue had got into her eyes
As she sat smoking some cheap cigar
In her motorized wheelchair
In front of the Presbyterian church
Her legs that had never ever perched
Hanging limp like scarecrow snakes

A homeless old invalid
Of the mightiest state
On the globe - the United States

Maples had turned purple
Birches golden yellow
In the church courtyard
With change of seasons
Yet, her eyes were smoky
A desolation ancient and dusky

Nature has no discipline
She should have seen
The anguish in the grey eyes
And paused for a while
Before smiling in glee

It was five in the evening
The cold was biting
Free dinner at the church
Was still two hours from thence
She complained, she should have patience
Till then, if she wished
To sleep on a half-filled stomach at least
Without disturbance

A visitor to the United States
I could only mouth some pleasantries
Say adieu and leave in a hurry

The grey eyes in despair remained
Fixed on a hapless sky
Which then decided to rain
Tear-drops in empathy down
On a homeless evening
That had no statehood
But a universal ache
Global and galactic

A distressed psyche wailed
Somewhere there with a dying bird
Was it a skylark, nightingale, who cares
In a world that has long gone destitute

50. Mount Rainier

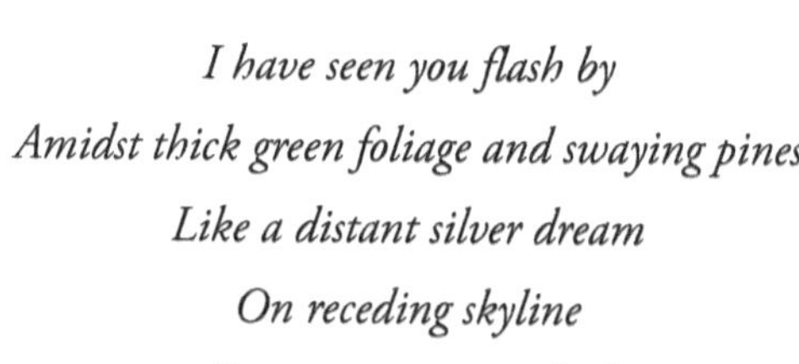

I have seen you flash by
Amidst thick green foliage and swaying pines
Like a distant silver dream
On receding skyline
But was never satisfied
For a close encounter I craved

I did then go up
The Space Needle in Seattle
Hoping to have a clear view
Of your snow-clad balding pate
That thought profound thoughts
Against mortal blues of the empty sky
But, alas, you remained
Elusive to sight
Hiding behind shifting clouds

Yesterday, I drove over a hundred miles
Climbed my way to Sunrise Point
Hoping for a close tete-a-tete
You played truant again
I saw a blank
Of nothingness, void
A grey screen of clouds and mist
As snow-flakes flew around
The board before me read
You were somewhere there
Amidst mighty peaks
Right before my unseeing eyes

Doesn't matter Rainier
You are there, I know for sure
Like the Himalayan peaks
I haven't seen
And yet am charmed by their beauty
On calendars, picture-cards
Inherent philosophy
Their height and grandeur speak

Better luck next time
Rainier, you are a teacher
I have now seen
Lofty nothingness, void
Against which I have all the peaks
Of the world that speak
Of Truth that belongs not to things
But to an evanescent dream
That the Lord, whoever He is
Conjures up for stupid minds

51. Antares of Hope

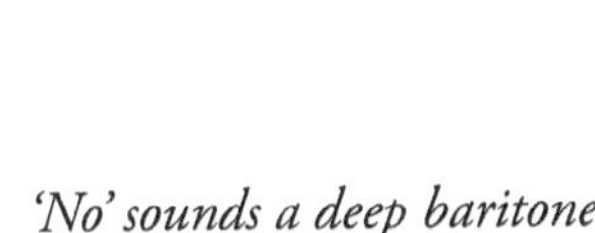

'No' sounds a deep baritone
And as India claps in unison
'No' it repeats in a deeper tone
Bachchan has returned
The towering Goliath
To deliver a blow of death
On feudal Indian male mind-set
That lays down dos and don'ts
Just only for women
While men can philander
Desecrate, defile, rape
Run amok like drunken apes
Doing what they want
Without control, unquestioned

A woman may do
All that men are accustomed to do
But yet when she says 'No'
That is the end
Beyond which no one should infringe
Roars Bachchan
With fire in his eyes
She may just be anybody
A girl-friend, your own wife
Mother or mate of somebody
A woman of loose morals
Whatever that means
But when she has said 'No'
Don't then place a step ahead

The thespian has returned
In a new avatar
Who in his young days personified
A messiah on screen
In whom oppressed Indian women
Multitudes of the less privileged
Unfortunate ones of Indian streets
Found a savior big brother or son

Indian womanhood now
Clings to his aging long arms to bow
In tearful gratitude
For speaking out for them
To a slumbering nation's conscience
In hard-hitting, no uncertain terms

The end of the night has come

A red giant has risen

In the Indian skies

A gigantic Antares of hope

A grateful nation wakes

To Bachchan's roar

That sends shivers down the spines

Of adamant, unheeding swine

52. Lives Gone Extinct without Heir

(This is my humble attempt at translating Mr. E.S. Unnikrishnan's beautiful Malayalam poem 'Anyam Ninnu Poya Jeevithangal)

The tribe of slates having gone forever
extinct without heir
*the poor eraser pepper elder**
stands waiting even today,
perplexed on the alleyway,
asking to school its way

**A plant the leaves of which school children of long ago used to erase writings on their slates.*

53. Sunset

There was a lush green redwood tree
Set against a brilliant winter sky
Of magnificent sunset
There was an unseen breeze
Whose presence
The movements of foliage bespoke
And there was that wood-pecker
Laboring on the dry finger
Of a dying cotton-wood

Who saw that?
A question of depth
Because I had lost myself
In that ethereal sight
I was beside myself
I was the tree, the sky
The sunset, breeze
Rustle of the leaves
Wood-pecker, cotton-wood
And the whole scene
One after the other
Till I asked the stupid question
"Who saw it? "

And with that my nascent ignorance

Is back with a vengeance

Then I am the one who saw

The seen are alien to me

I saw the scene

With my eyes

Threatened by an impending cataract

Oh, I am to see the doc

Next day morning

A being that likes

To languish bound in misery

Despite the freedom of beautiful sunsets

That it encounters and loses itself

At least once in a while

54. Over the Bamboo Fence

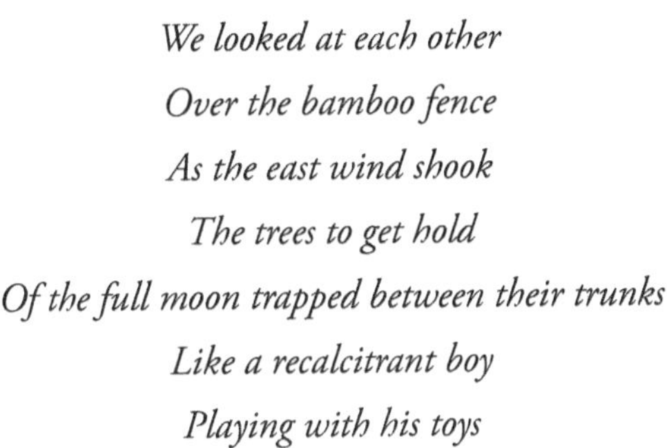

We looked at each other
Over the bamboo fence
As the east wind shook
The trees to get hold
Of the full moon trapped between their trunks
Like a recalcitrant boy
Playing with his toys

Two hours yet to go
Before the sun rose
Your eyes then shone like stars
And I stood watching them
Across the fence
Uttered not we a word
But yet said all that there was to be said

Thank you for that memory, dear
Every time the trees capture the moon
In their swaying hold
I see your smiling face
And the stars shining in your eyes
No matter where you are now
Dead or alive
Oh, do lovers ever die?

55. Deception Falls

On Stevens pass
We had a stop
At Deception Falls
In the thick green alpine growth
Home for ubiquitous, instant moss

A brook violent, impulsive, young
Cascades here and roars her way down
Against mighty boulders of stones
She can put several tons
Of weight to crush any animal resistance
Out of mortal existence

And then slowly ages down her path
To be serene, calm and quiet
Where she meets
The river Tye
Like the Tao of the East
Her last refuge
When fingers
Can play a note on her
Soft as if on a guitar

Strange things aging does to restless ones
I looked at a sagely Douglas fir
A presiding giant on her banks for an answer
Who has perhaps walked down the path of fire
A couple of centuries before
When a forest conflagration or volcanic eruption
Changed the ecological face of the place
Beyond recognition

He beckoned me
To sit at his feet
Under his saintly gaze
And meditate
Covered all over by moss
Like a green man
Unearthly from Mars
Envied by other smaller trees
That pined for the light of the sun
Bent their way away from his spreading arms

Like the sage of ancient Indian lore
Valmiki, on whom ants built their hill*
As he sat through ages pondering
Answers to profound existential worries

Oh, my limbs are already growing moss
May it grow deep into my bones
On this hillside of great symbiosis
May I hibernate here and meditate
A moss-man chrysalis listening to the gushing brook
My way unto the stars
And beyond them into the unknown
Land of fluttering butterflies

---

*Valmiki is the Indian sage who authored the epic Ramayana. He was a hunter-robber in early life.

56. Lonely Star

A lonely star
This August night
Who are you?
I can't figure out
With all my knowledge of the night sky

At a place several thousand miles
From mine
Where I don't know
Which is east and west
Who are you
Staring at me this lonely night
At me in my armchair
Eyes fixed on the dome above?

Whoever you are
We have been together
Through distant ages
Our unfamiliarity now
Conceals a closeness
Through several eons

Star you are
In my bosom dome
I have been looking at you
From cradle till now
You will be there over my grave
Staring at me when the dew
Struggles to hold on to grass-blade tips
In the ground frost at my funeral ground

Oh what a sweet knowing that is
The dew, the grass, the star and me
All together in close embrace!
Has life ever been sweeter than this?!

57. Planet of the Chimps

Grandson's first birth-day
His cousins arrived
Twin girls half his age
Two is company, three is a crowd

Middle of the night
The three screamed
From different nooks of the house
Like sympathetic detonation
Call of gastric fire
Or was it diaper rash?

Moms and grandmas scampered
Mixing milk in bottles
Singing lullabies
In unknown tongues
Music illiterates
How silly! Can music ever douse
The raging fire of hunger
A burning hidden sore?
Screams just got louder

The men now joined
Sleep-walking dads and grandpas
Their hair disheveled
Pajama strings swaying loose
Like pendulums of grandpa clocks
Former music school terrors
Outdid the women in notes
Kids screeched without reprieve

Pandemonium prevailed for a while
The chimps then dozed off in a milky high
With bottles in their delicate hold
Moms, dads, grands tip-toed
Finger on lips, scared
As if in a mine-field
Speaking in hush-hush mode
Lest the tykes are roused
Again in unison screamed

Oh, what a scene that was!
Tyranny of the babes!
The whole littered house
A planet of the chimps!
Eh you, wash the bottles
You there, change my pads and bibs!

58. Immortality

Change is known against unseen permanence
Finitude against the concept of fullness
As ignorance cries out to omniscience
Life seeks out immortality
While time rivers sequentially into eternity

Someone taught me
The latter in all these is the same
And I am truly the latter
Transient all the former

Birds that sing and die in the bush
Winds breathing their last stopped by mounts
Flowers that smile in the sun and wither at night
Spring-time streams that dry up in the heat
Galaxies spinning into black-hole mouths
All of them transient asked me aloud:

What are we and where are we
In the grand schematology
Of your pompous immortality?

Head bent, shamed by their poser
I knew they were the very mirror
In which I saw my fullness
Complete if I am, a mirror
Outside me is sure an error
They are in me, so never apart
Immortal, all in one
The non-dual song of eternity
We can sing only together
Never alone, never alone!

59. Bothell in Meditation

An overworked Sun sank himself

In twilight red wine

Bothell sat to meditate

As birds retired, stopped singing

It was a musky dusk of August

Somewhere in the darkening woods

A solitary bleeding heart

Burnt incense

Honeysuckles drooped in prayer

Evening traffic roared

On the roads in haste

Throbbing arteries of Bothell

But, despite the apparent roar

She found silence

Sat rooted in herself

Like a ship that has dropped the weight of its anchor

Into the bottom of bottomlessness

Unburdened melting away

In the hue of an ethereal sunset

Conifers of different genres
Scaled against the glow
Of the dying day
Into the void
Like thoughts that are just witnessed
Without being followed
Vanish like flames that seek
And die in the air of nothingness

Oaks stood ruminating
Their gigantic frames
Seeking the essence of inner evanescence
Birches, maples, dogwoods, firs
Stood in hushed silence
Finger on their lips
In attendance, ever attentive
Before their meditating madam

Bothell sat meditating
Lost in herself
The seed from which sprouted
All that happened around
Trees, sky, the scent of flowers
The evening hue and the stars
Like a colorful umbrella that unfolds
On to existence from nothingness
At every batting of the eyelids

60. Missing Button

Eh, today on the walkway
Of this pretty town near Seattle
My wife lost a unique, colorful button
Of an exotic top she bought
At some incense-smelling boutique
In the Arabian Gulf

Prodded by her I set on
To search for the missing button
Following her doggedly
Back the walkway
My head bent all along
Looking for the precious loss

Passers by smiled at me
Said 'Hi'
Neither did I hear nor did I see
An uncommunicative Indian
Conifers and maples on the road side
Smiled I didn't see
The setting sun, his face down
Sunk sulking at the indifferent me

A world was lost for a fool
Looking for a button
That fastened a mortal bosom
Like I lost long ago
A whole world
When a love cast me to the winds
And went her way
Leaving me trapped
Ruminating and ruing a stupid loss
Over tear-wet pillows
Missing beautiful sunsets
Talkative birds, trees and hills
All the while
Oh, such is life
Get up and enjoy ye stupid

61. To Each His Own

A well-to-do boy once screeched
To a poor one on the street
He could view the entire town
From his condo at the top
Of a high-rise on a hill
Where affluent of the city dwelt

The slum-dog couldn't visualize
The privileges of the rich
Far beyond his reach
Yet, he smiled, for he could see
Through his broken, leaky roof
The star farthest and the moon

The stars above his hut demurred
Thought let us try his wits again
Your sight is nothing boy
Look at us, don't we high above you see
Galaxies in eternal spin
In our never-ending night

The boy's reply was a poser
That paled their stellar demeanor
Oh, stars have you ever seen
A rainbow, I have several ones

Be happy with your own
It is said 'to each his own'
To each a window has been given
Watch through it to heart's content
Never for a moment lament

62. Spider Bhai! Good Morning!

Every time my naughty grandson
Who is just about one
Goes cranky, throws a tantrum
I have noticed
A peek into the open soothes him

He likes the trees
Tall verdant maples and pines
Against the dark blue sky
The glisten of their leaves
Wandering lonely clouds
And the breeze on his indignant cheeks

Yet, often all these tranquilizers fail
When there is a little savior at the door
A small spider who does the trick
Whom we greet every morn
"Spider Bhai! Good Morning! "

We have let our guest live
And rule his almost invisible net in peace
Every time my finger pokes
He retreats deep into the web
The kid then beams with a smile

Lowering himself from my shoulder
He then tries his own finger on the spider
Eyes shine in joy, wet cheeks dry
As the arachnid plays hide and seek
A baby cackle then breaks

Is it not strange
That when arachnophobia plagues
Almost every naked ape
That walks the earth calling itself human
A child is enamored by a domestic weaver!
Where does their communion originate?

Aren't we created to live in peace
Without fear, in love and ease?
And then do we err down the drain
That we call growing
To fear and hate all other beings?

May our babies inherit
A world where no phobias exist
It is in them to make that dream
And let us teach them sing
"Spider Bhai! Good Morning! "

Note: "Bhai" in Hindi means brother.

63. Birthday Party

I sat watching them
Scamper, gather, chatter
Across the party hall
Filled plates in hands
Noodles and spaghetti
Drooling from their overworked lips
And getting drawn in again
With spicy technical jargon

Young techies in their twenties
Girls and boys
Hired by a software giant
From Bangalore, Hyderabad, Pune
And distant Gurgaon
At a child's birthday party
In Seattle where drizzles played
Peek-a-boo hide and seek
With a reluctant sun

Theirs was a world
Far away, perhaps, by light years
From my sunset senility
Is a generation so far away?
I heard them I thought
But didn't hear a word
As they spoke
Every movement of their lips
Escaped my comprehension
A clouded tearful afternoon

They talked and talked
Exchanged pleasantries
Discussed their work and woes
As I sat looking at them blank
Like shoals of fish in frenetic motion
Oft breaking apart and scattering
In cackles of mirthful laughter

The party went on
In the hall of my awareness
Guests trickled in and out
Till my stare was stark empty
Silence prevailed

What did it matter
If I heard them or not
If I had my hearing aid on
All that counted
The party happened
In my presence
The presence I am
The happening's very essence

64. Blinking Monkey

There is a doll of a monkey
In the toilet
My daughter assigned
For my use in her Seattle home

The monkey seems to blink
Every time I use the commode
She has a baby hugging her shoulder
Which also seems to blink

Blink, blink, blink
At the often inebriate me
Who encroaches your privacy
Meandering into your home
The toilet - your private abode

Reminding me of a distant past
When I roamed the forest
A Neanderthal, the missing link
Homo erectus, a yelling ape
God knows what

Oh doll, I am an ape
Incurable, inebriate
Thanks I am reminded of it
Every time I am inside the toilet
Blink, blink and blink
May Darwin rest in peace
And the monkey in me ease

65. Jet Lag

A somnambulistic streak
Ringing in the head
Nerves frayed
Eyelids heavy
Through alleys
Of blinking awareness
Island worlds
Patches of grey
Pitch-darkness and glitter
Apparent reals
Broken into pieces
After a straight hurtle
Across several zones of time
In a matter of half a day

A broken mirror
No distinction whatever
Between the pieces
What is dream stuff
So-called waking world
Sliding into each
Through vertical chutes
Of fast transit
As cicadas screech
Circadian alarms scream
Yet no up or down
No hill or plain
Only sonorous snore
At exit, entry doors

Names and forms
Dissipate, coalesce
Clouds in whirl
Hebephrenic thoughts
Incoherent abstract
Every fallacy is right
Worlds in march
In parallel cascade

A mammoth pachyderm
Struggling without luck
Out of a gigantic mud-pit
Onto seeming land
Of solid respite
Where there are
Asylums, alas, for mental wrecks
Peopled by the wise
Who have burnt their lives
On Freud, Jung and the like

66. Eid in Dubai

The weatherman says
"It is 42 Celsius
Feels like 54"
The city swelters
Covered all over
By a humid blanket
Its abounding skyscrapers
Looming heavenwards
Like skeletal apparitions
Transfixed in a haze

It is Eid in Dubai
The wondrous city
That for many is paradise
Labourers and the moneyed alike
Who have just finished
Month-long day-time fasting
To usher in festivities

Summer smells everywhere
Of dust on the road and in the air
Like camphorous drunkenness
In buses, cars and metro trains

Oblivious of the discomfort
Multitudes move about
Like ants, chasing far-away dreams
Their gaze lost to distant thoughts
Of wives, kids and families
Across nooks and corners of the globe

As the sun sinks and the day gasps
They emerge in hordes from labour camps
Scurry across roads for daily needs
To overcrowded supermarkets
And on to parks that dot the city
To lie on the grass
Sweat and dream all the way to the stars

They are the worker-bees
Who impart humming life
To the gigantic beehive
The city called Dubai

Cacophonous Bengalis
Sinewy Pakistanis
Chirping Filipinos
Ubiquitous Indians
And several nationalities
They make a miracle work
With the precision of a machine

And where is the queen bee
Who has them leashed?
No one sees
Other than on TVs
The masters on whose command
The machine is made to work
They are nowhere conspicuous
What one sees everywhere
Are the worker-bees
In humming sprees
All happily provided

Long live Dubai
May peace always prevail
May it always be
Eid in this wondrous paradise
The like of which
Nowhere on this globe exists

67. Body

Watch, watch, watch
My limbs move
My body moves
I am neither the movements
Nor am the body
For am just the watcher
For I just happen to see
The body and its movements
Thanks to what nobody knows

"No, no, no
That can't be true"
Someone said
From inside me
Oh, what inside! ?
No clue where that someone is lodged
Yet, I know someone said
If that is someone and if I knew
I can't then be him
I am the knower in the game

A mosquito bit
On my knee
My eyes were closed
Yet, in my mental eye
I could see
My knee with the mosquito on
Even the colour of what I wore

But that had nothing to do
With my actual attire then
When what there really was
Only the experience of a bite
A flash or flowering
In the awareness that I am
Like a ripple in a lucid pond

My knee that was bitten
And the attire I saw
Were just an image
Gathered from the past
Down memory lane

The body is a thought
Never is it wholly felt
But only in bits and parts
Nose, eyes, ache or ease
Then as a whole conjured up
Like a group photograph

The knee thus I know
Is an unwanted add-on
On the singular flash
That was just a bite
An experience, a knowing
Flash of consciousness
Which I always am
Through all transactions
Which fools christen
The world or the universe
Of names and forms

May Consciousness only shine
Nay it is the only One that shines
Which I am
There is then nothing else
The world is Consciousness
A single whole
Perceived as impossible parts
The seer I am
Never different from it

What a tragedy then
That I am wont
To always see it split into parts
Diverse, different
Often as a looming threat

68. Cheryl

Sweating in the summer Sun of Dubai
My shopping trolley overloaded
I struggled at my building door
When she, a kid of hardly seven
Beaming, held it open for me to pass

As we meandered towards the lifts
She in front like an angel in brisk steps
That hardly touched the floor
I asked her what she was named

'Cheryl' came the answer
Then she chirped how old she was
In which class she studied
From Mangalore she hailed
The little mass of condensed confidence

Inside the lift I wanted to know
What she would like to be
Pat came the answer
'A teacher' and the reason for the wish
'There are poor kids in my land
Who need my help with their lessons'

From her poised air of assurance
Polished shine and countenance
I had thought she would name
Fashion designing for a career
Or follow in the footsteps
Of astronaut Sunita Williams
Or at least a doctor highly specialized
Working in the United States

Her answer had me bowled over
A sob blocked my throat
As I stood behind her
Struggling to hold back tears
Of joy - a wasteland of seventy
Dwarfed by a mere tiny seven

Oh, how fortunate is my motherland
A little brave-heart here burns
For her, in the cradle of comforts and riches
A midnight candle of love and hope
A thousand miles away from her shores
Cheryl dear, crores of kids may you inspire

69. Agony and Ecstasy

Clouds cumulus, cumulonimbus
Looked from behind the peaks
Of the Western Ghats

They smelt Monsoon
Trade winds that set ships
Inspired by a legendary visage
Which blazed many a male solar plexus
The Helen of Troy

Helens walked the Tamil streets
Their saris fluttering in the wind
Soaked in odoriferous sweat
An evening intoxicated

Neems shook their heads
In demoniac frenzy
A dance of the dames
Of the Arabian Gulf
Scent of sweat and oud
Intermixed to rouse
The passions of the yearning young

Let me lie here inebriate
To capture the beauty of this state
Of ecstasy that pervades
Every atom of my being

Beautiful is life
Beautiful are the Helens
May a thousand ships
Set sail again

My solar plexus aches
In an agony that is sweet
Agony and ecstasy
Oh, how blazing is this corporeal being
Of everyone of us slowly dying
Whoever said the body is a thing! ?

70. How, Cow, Bou!

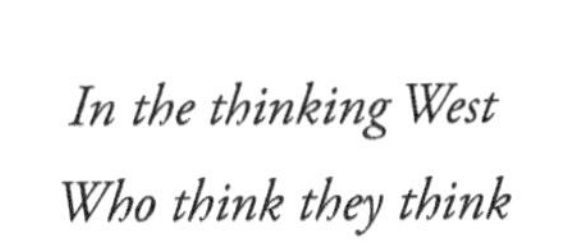

In the thinking West
Who think they think
It is always how and how
They worry how things work

In my India
It is always cow and cow
They conceive and sanctify
An udder that never fails
To deliver all their needs

And in a few other places
It is a lot of bou and bou
Loud barks that clamor
To be heard at all nooks and corners

71. She

She stood under the neem tree
Swayed by the west wind
This summer night
As mercury soared ambitious heights

The lonely street light
With cataract sight
Shone her matted coppery hair
Tattered attire

She stood there
Like a wisp of air
Exuding sweat's sweet odour
Feathery delicate
An apparition whose feet
Seemed to shun the earth
Like angels in flight

Yet, she was a woman
With all her privations
As earthly as everyone
A daughter, wife or sister
An embodiment that fired
Reactions in those who beheld

Oh, vagabond west wind
Protect her from hurt
She is a poet's pet
Whether or not she wept
Sweated, cried in fright
Or perished unnoticed

Woman lives on
Under looming trees
In alleys of despair
Mother, sister, daughter
No one cares to bother

72. Narcissuses

They sat on either side
Of the walkway
Dozing catatonics
Fixated to smart phone screens
Some happy, some unhappy
With their own clumsy selfies

In saturnine pose
Curled up
Like Narcissus of yore
Enamored by his own image
On the placid waters of a pool

As crumbling walkers
Walked and walked
To distant health hidden
Somewhere on receding horizons
Earphones plugged
Into their ears
Looks dazed into yonder skies
Unaware of what was on
Around the walking streak
Listening to music
Or what amused
A beloved's chirp
Hymns, spiritual burp

A world lost to technology
Sound and sight
Sans any soul
Inner abode or eye

People of straw
Like a summer drizzle
Who can't a world make
Abounding on the outside
That, alas, has no inside
Losing themselves to the tricks
Of the stealthy seductress
Technological advance

Or is it all wrong?
Is this the way species evolve?
Darwin may have the last laugh

These zombies may at last
Evolve and long last
In a scenario we can't forecast
A lotos land of the lost
Where it is always afternoon
With no night or forenoon
As flowers in full bloom
God, please give them the Moon

73. Screams, Fear and Panic

Last year
They blasted a city square
Exulted in a bath of gore
That was Paris
Our eyes are still wet

And now
They are doing a repeat
At Brussels
The airport is all gore
Screams, fear and panic

And at my feeble doorsteps
Thousands of miles apart
Wayward youngsters
Self-styled intellectuals
Anointed living martyrs
Are clamoring for freedom
Extolling despicable icons
In acts of vandalism

Freedom from what we ask
In dismay, it turns out
Freedom from the freedom we have

God help us this world
If that is in your unfortunate mandate
Yet, we bow our heads
In thanksgiving and eternal hope
The lot of lost mankind
That still believes
In sanity amidst unthinkable madness

74. I Am a Song That Never Stops to Sing

This evening I prayed
To the Mother of the Universe
Ma, get into my veins
My nerves and skin
And sing, sing and sing

She just smiled
As She ever does
The unfailing Mother
And here I am trying to sing
In sheer abandon

On a sultry evening
When friendly west winds
Have begun their amorous strokes
On the heads of sleeping palms
Across the plains
Against crimson skies

That have imbued into them
The hope of impending rains
Sing, sing, west wind
Sing you the lonely bird
That seeks a nest for the night
To hatch an egg
That breaks out next morn
In a universal song

The world is indeed beautiful
Grant me Ma discerning eyes
And a mind that can sing
Your eternal songs in ceaseless strains

A singer here I am
Who can't sing
Unyielding vocal cords
Yet, your song reverberates
In the silent skies
Of my thoughts
Through the bird
The hatching egg
And the stars who guard the nest

Sing, sing and sing
That is all I can do
Through everything that is a thing
That can sing
Ma You are nonpareil
It doesn't matter
If my vocal cords have failed

The song still comes along
Gushing out through so many blessed things
The whole world is a song
Who cares if it is a cuckoo
Or a quail that sings
Whoever said I can't sing
When everything that I am is a song
I am a song that never stops to sing

75. First Summer Shower

She came

Without a warning

This afternoon

I had snoozed

In the sultry summer heat

She clapped her hands

In a thunder bolt

Startled I awoke

Or so I thought

My neck and chest

In a paroxysm of sweat

And there she was

The first summer rain

Dancing on roof-tops

To a music

That only silly gods conceive

I lay there unable to move

My limbs in motor paralysis

Beautiful is her dance

Let her perform

The distant mountains smelt

In the wafting winds

Of herbs, earth and forlorn love

And this night

I would sleep

My face pressed

Into a smelly pillow

Her dark locks

That smell a primeval past

Thank you summer rain

You are a dream

In which seeds buried conceive

A greenery and dreams

That man can never ever deserve

76. God

The dilapidated atheist sat
Self-proclaimed rationalist
Fondling his smoky beard
Eyes myopic, looks haggard
Laboring with tons of knowledge
That loaded his swollen head
Case of intellectual encephalitis

A sign-board on his desk read
'There is no God' - the goddamned word
He said should be removed
From all dictionaries the kids read
So they grew up true rationalists
Excelled as great scientists

An untouched fat tome covered with dust
Adorned a corner of his desk
Oxford, Chambers, or Webster,
God knows whatever
Perhaps, a volume of the great Britannica
That carried knowledge without measure
By which he always swore
Except for that one unfortunate word
'God', which he was convinced
Shouldn't exist, for God doesn't exist

His life now almost expended
In negating sadly what he was convinced
Never ever existed
He was feared by the pious
None dared debate with him
Invincible he strode
Like Fagin of Dickens
Triumphant, villainous, grinning
Hands inserted in his trouser pockets

Till a guy, stupid in his eyes,
Shot a poser - why not identify
Other things that don't exist
And have them too prised
Away from the books children read

Fagin fumed with scorn
Dumb-ass, go ahead mention
Just one other thing that should be thrown
Into the bin with your unwanted icon

Nonchalant answered the stupid
Permanence is first in my list
Show me a thing that forever exists
In a universe where even stars perish
More such words then I can enlist

Caught on wrong foot, Fagin thought,
This dumb-ass he shouldn't underrate
Cautious now he explained
Permanence can remain
For it is just a concept, an antonym,
For the impermanence the world suffers

Heat and cold I can accept
Light and darkness as well,
Stupid rejoined, as antonyms,
For the pairs very much exist
So is the case with happiness
And all our unhappiness,
For both do we experience
How in the world, tell me, Sir,
Do you accept what doesn't exist
As antonym for a fact plaguing our midst?

What logic permits you
To accept non-existent impossibilities
Into your reasoning sensibilities
Like immortality and omniscience
Fullness and omnipotence
When all that you have for keeps
Is death, change, limitation and weakness?

And why does your maths
Yearn to embrace the impossible lass
Who is christened infinity
When all it has are numbers
Playing finitudinal chess
And counting pebbles like Newton said?

Fagin sat speechless
He knew he had to trash
With God, a lot of his erstwhile vocabulary
All the words the dumb-ass arrayed
Which he had shamelessly used
In his innumerable debates
With eminent adversaries

The simpleton closed the debate
Giving Fagin a parting kick
It is immortality against which you rue
Your time-bound mortality
As every change that occurs in time
Is seen against an unchanging screen
It is omniscience against which shines
Your silly knowledge and ignorance
And it is fullness that lights up
The falsity of your limited being
All your wants and inadequacies

Without the three you can't be
The world can't be
The three are non-different
And synonyms for the God you trash
As is permanence which you can't spot
And yet not do away with

The day this Truth is realized
Reckon you are no more you
The failing corpus, but one with God
Nay, there is nothing else then but God
Against Whom the world does seem
Afflicted by birth and death
Change, wants and ignorance
For which reason He is called
The Creator with the magic wand
Now tell me if you want God trashed
Mind you then you too are trashed

Fagin sat stroking his beard
A bruised ego licked its sores
A perennial malady for atheists
All confounded rationalists

* 201 *

77. Death of a Crane

It was a Devi temple
In my native town
Where I had the darshan of the Devi
The Mother of the Universe

Decked in flowers
Bejeweled, She was all smiles
Lighted by lamps
Mother Supreme
Triumphant to the rhythmic
Beating of the drums
Cymbals and bells
Noisy prayers
Of her innumerable lambs

When I ventured out
Of the temple, there on a concrete slab
Was a dying crane
In line with the temple door
And the flag-staff of Her valor

Perhaps shot by a merciless gunner
Poisoned or stricken
By some avian plague unknown

Heaped in a tragic feathery mess
Her white winged body
And black legs were already dead and stiff
What remained perhaps alive
Against the onslaught of ants
Were her eyes, yellow-rimmed
Her beak again yellow and a moving head

Which turned in protest
Against my stroking fingers
But relented in silence
On my persistence
To the universal empathy
That binds the commune
Of helpless beings
Everywhere globally
And galactically

I went back again
Into the temple
Where Her sanctum sanctorum
Was closed for the last prayers
Of the forenoon

And I prayed standing there
A mass of tears
Not for my own material benefit
Not for those of my ilk
But for the dying crane
That had my heart gashed and bleeding

The puja was over
Temple door opened
Mother smiled Her adieu
For the forenoon
On Her devotees
In absorbed genuflection

Bells rang aloud
As ecstasy gushed
Across the spines
Of Her milling lambs
Heaped in prostration
On the granite floor

And as I looked out
I saw the head
Of the crane had stilled
Mother had it sure taken
To Her abode of everywhere
Leaving the grieving me
In tearful desperation
With faltering steps
As though drunk
In a world of clouds
Rain, heat and swelter
Oh, how I wish
I had been that crane!

Shoot me please
If you don't mind
So that I can be the crane
On the concrete slab
When She reappears and beams
At Her evening return
To Her milling devotees

Cloud, wind or rain
Can you hear me please
The wailing me
That longs to be a crane?

78. Diwali Remembrance

She had simian features
But burning eyes
Mostly in chemise
She was adrenaline
That set my heart in spate

That was long long ago
When we shared company
In the flash of Diwali crackers
And roaring sparklers
All that I remember
She smelt too good
In her teenage efflorescence

I hadn't then seen
Arabian beauties
Or ogled the blondes
Brunettes, blacks
That set Hollywood on fire
With cleverly concealed anatomical features

Sophia Loren was unknown
As was Irma La Douce
Ursula was yet to bewitch
Robbers in forlorn deserts

She lent me the fire
With which I lighted crackers
Most of which misfired
Each time the light was passed
I saw her eyes glint
In a primeval fire
That spread out a night-sky of stars

Having lost her forever
In my senility now
I need only the memory of that fire
To light my crackers
And sporadic sparklers
Through lonely nights
Like comets in spate

Oh, Diwali is a splendour
May I have her around
In her scanty chemise
Smelling all time good
Like a haystack in rain wet
Or at least a memory of it

79. Diwali Thoughts

The night ended to greet the morn
As the world around
Boomed and flared
With Diwali fire

The morning wind
Reeked cracker fumes
Wandered lazily around
Over rain-soaked earth
As children roared
In fun and mirth

Kitchens that had worked
Late into night woke again
Early in the morn
To dress up or season
Their day-and-night toil
Of savouries and sweets
And arrange them
In gleaming vessels
And on sprawling plates

As women still wet after their bath
Adorned jasmine on their hair
As they draped silk
Over their bare sandalwood torsos
A TV channel blared
The thousand names
Of the Mother
Of The Universe
With Her mighty image
Seated on a lion
Brightening the screen

A wise man in saffron
His forehead ashen
Stoked his beard
On another channel
His eyes glistening
As he expounded
Profound philosophical truths
From some sacred Sanskrit scripture

A lady activist on another one
Who perhaps had no childhood
Nor seen the glint in the eyes
Of a tot holding a lighted sparkler
Lamented the pollution of the festival
Warned everyone of global warming
And sought a Green Diwali
Sans sound, light and play

Yet another one had a lady
Flamboyant with patchy eyes
Perhaps hyperlipidaemic
Who dished out recipes
Of sautéed chicken with honey
And a salad of dried shrimps
At six in the morning
To her audience sipping tea
Over unbrushed teeth

Another channel aired
A Tamil remake
Of a Hindi thriller
Where the hero flexed his musculature
Splashed gore wherever he went
Overdoing his Hindi counterpart
Like a blazing comet in close orbit

Men on their morning stroll
Paused to greet one another
And debated the harm
The boom, light and sound
Caused to animals and birds
As crows over their head
Seated on a swaying palm
Cawed in utter disdain

An India of diversity
In the abandon of Diwali felicity
Where each had a vision
Where each was right or wrong
According to perceptions
Mixed in a turmoil
In a democratic whirlpool
A fearsome Charybdis

I sat there watching
The din, light and cacophony
Looking at just one lamp
Amidst the thousands of Diwali
That burnt a golden wick
Along the universal spine
Where the noise and light
Melted into naught
In a silence which said
All are not
But just one and that is all

Here I remain an Indian to the hilt
And that is what makes me and my nation click
HAPPY DIWALI TO ALL!

80. To the Mountain Breeze

Mountain breeze!
Please pause
To console this aching landscape
At the foot of the hill
Lost in transcendental thrill

We the inhabitants of the plains
Know that you originate
In the skies where the clouds of mortal worries
Don't navigate
Above where
The head of the great mount resides

Yet, please do come
Sweep our lonely homes
We, the coughing ones
On sinking easy-chairs
Breathe your natural aroma
The smell of the skies
Clouds, mountain herbs
That are renowned
To kill mortal ills
And put our asthmatic psyche
At perpetual ease

Please do come breeze
This is a call from one
Who has seen in you
A constant companion
Fondly stroking the hair
On his vexed forehead
Sweating attire
From kindergarten days

Here in my senility I lie
Unsung, drained of life
Please do come
So we can sing
A carol or a bhajan
To whatever that makes things click
On this barren land of dreams

Please do come mountain breeze
On my knees am I
In supplication
In my dying caravanserai
Of brittle mortal bones
Ebbing senses and feels
On a lonely desert plain

81. Diwali Celebrity

Things changed all of a sudden
With greetings and acknowledgements
Pouring in from unfamiliar directions
I have become
A celebrity overnight

The security men at the gate
Stooped into my car
With a loud "Good Morning, Sir"
The launderer who irons our clothes
The milkman and the paper-boy
And the grumpy car cleaner
Who cleans the neighbour's vehicles
The guy at the parking lot
Of the supermarket
God knows what he does
The uncaring beggar on the streets
Have all overnight turned over-polite
Acknowledging my so far unnoticed
Insignificant existence

The watchmen at our neighbouring villas
Who demanded my identity to be proved
The other day to access their premises
Jumped in front of my car
Precariously to wish me a good day

The cat was out when the young maid
At my friend's apartment
Who blushes and hangs her head
At my greying masculinity
Was emboldened today
To smile and look into my eyes
And pronounce in no uncertain terms
"Happy Diwali to you, Sir, and madam"

Oh, I am a celebrity today
Who the world has time to accept
Thanks to Diwali
Who cares about tomorrow
All celebrities have to go

82. King Kong

I am King Kong
The primal angst
Where is my Ann?
Place her on my palm
Ye pigmy brutes
That try to vanquish
A lover with your skirmishes
Planes, ammunitions, guns
On the heights of insanity
This high-rise Empire State edifice

Look at the wrinkles on my face
The fire in my eyes
Shudder ye little brutes
Who have lighted
A perineal fire
Down on my spine
Down in my being
I want my Ann
Where is she?
Place her on my palm

So I look at her beautiful face
And then at the golden sunset
With an inner ache
Joy concentrate
Glands ablaze
In primordial bliss

Oh, why have you shown
This garden of Eden?
Having eaten the forbidden fruit
I can't now leave
Unless death puts me to sleep

Sweet is this pain
Sweet is the glow
That enrapture my being
Give me my Ann
With her on my palm
Let me go down
The primal lover
On the altar of his love
Shot into smithereens
By insipid fools

Beautiful is the sunset
Me the brute has it said
Beauty and the beast
Are never apart
A lover here groans
Before he withers
Shot into bits
By brutish might

83. I Walked a Tamil Street

I waked a Tamil street

Inebriate

On an October evening

When a cloud hesitated overhead

Unable to rain

Lost in thoughts

Perhaps, God knows what

The North East monsoon is playing hide and seek

The weather bureau said

What could they say

About a thing unknown?

When forecasts go wrong

There are excuses numberless

That shelter and comfort

The evenings swelter

A lonely star, perhaps Sirius
Or Betelgeuse
From behind the clouds
Looked down on the street
Where two buxom beauties
Rushed on a scooter
Loaded with jasmine on their heads
To unknown beds
Infested with bugs
To share carnal pleasures
With their sweating boyfriends

A barking stray dog
His eyes wary
Sought friendship
Of everyone on the street
Wagging his tail

Men and women
Walked up and down
As in a dream
Oh, how humans could be
So somnambulist
In so much physical discomfort!

That is life
When ignorance drives
Why should men be any wise?
An unwanted demand
Of those who think themselves high

May I therefore seek
My bed of bugs
Somewhere here
Comforted by a solitary breeze
This October night
Watched by lonely stars
With friendly barks
Jasmine, sweat, beauties
Life needless to say
Is always beautiful
Who cares here to breathe the last
Unless that is thrust upon?

84. Col. Gaddafi

Muammar,
You were a violent passion
Long ago in my Bombay days
When we jostled with crowds
Singing praise for Nasser, Arafat and you
We felt we shared
A common vision
A shapeless glorious morn

It didn't matter if our stomachs burnt
It didn't matter if the skies poured
As long as our young blood roared
We headed in swarming hordes
To meetings held on city roads
To cheer and clap leaders of the Left
The Middle-East then beckoned our hearts

We held your pictures close to chest
A guard of honour by armed cadets
Men whose muscles spoke your might
With uniformed girls in perfect file
Saluting their leader heads held high
And blue eyes filled with gleaming steel

Muammar,
You were a violent passion
A spinning electric storm
Powered by your hatred for colonists
You made your people dream
Feverishly in fits
Like they never had done
As you strode the land
A colossus in triumphant march
Building ambitious projects
Oft challenging the West
Thrilling your socialist friends

But you never knew
The masses dreamt too much
Then your revolution turned ruthless
Maverick without reason
Intolerant of dissent
Recklessly extravagant
Megalomaniac decadent

You never imagined
Their dreams were imbued
With seeds
Of a distant Arab Spring
That spelt your doom
In an uprising
They no more needed
A leader who donned
Atrocious attire at every whim
Like his myriad million moods

Till at last the fire of their fury
Fueled by your detractors globally
Burnt your mighty fortresses away
And drove you to the wilderness of Sirte
Close to where you first saw the light of day

Till they pulled you out of a pipe
Mauled and hauled you along the streets
In public view
A bullet then sufficed
Without regrets
To put an end to history
Glorious revolution gone awry

Muammar,
How much we wish
It hadn't happened that way
So that the sands and winds of Sirte
Could ever roar
To wanderers of the desert:
"And here lies our Muammar,
The King of Kings, Ozymandias-like,
Who taught the Libyans to dream;
Look on his works, ye mighty and despair"
Oh, that was not to be
Stark so is human tragedy.

85. Let Us India Make

A cruel taxi driver in Mumbai
Forced a Muslim woman
Out of his vehicle
For she was in labour
Providence had it that
She meandered into a Hindu temple
Of Lord Ganesh
Gave birth to a yelling
Full-throated Indian babe
Assisted by female devotees
Who had thronged the place
News says the child was named Ganesh

Another news items blares
Badly needed space was granted
At a Hindu temple in Mumbai
For Muslims to pray
On the day of Eid Al-Adha

Both incidents are in order
That is the way the world should be
No matter what brainless crooks say
Yet why is it that so much is said
About what every man should do
To his fellow human
And why does it become big news

When someone repairs a broken sparrow
Or pauses to sit beside
A dying cat to pray
Or rescues a stray dog from a well
All unnoticed, unreported

Man has it in him
A God that expresses often
In an elating empathy
May such men
Hold their hands together
And do an India make
Others will sure join
For elation is everyone's like
In sheer tears of joy

*Let them sing Vande Maataram**
Children born to a mother
Spanning miles and miles
Of beautiful earth
Enriched by the Ganges
Her eyes fixed on the sky
Of stars and galaxies
Listening for eons and eons
To the songs of universal love

Make India, make India
You sons of India
We are born at a Ganesha mosque
Or is it a church or a Jain temple
A gurudwara, it is all the same
Providence has it so
Lucky we remain
Singing Vande Maataram
In unison
As the dumbfounded stars listen

———————————

**salute the mother*

86. To Die Watched by God

Intubated I lay for air
Connected to a ventilator
For many days under others' care
At their mercy, on intravenous drip
Its bottle hanging over my head
Like a Damocles' sword
On enteral diet tube-fed

I am past ninety
I had a minor fall when my chair tipped
Broke my femur
The X-Ray said
The reason they grabbed
And dragged me to their abattoir
"Screw up the bone" they said
"The guy should walk again
If he doesn't, at least let us gain"

I didn't walk, I lay
Anaesthesia walked a long way
Carrying me like a sleeping babe
And when I awoke at last
I heard them say
"The guy has fever
Send his urine for culture
Put him on a course
Of the latest germ killer
Toxic it may be, doesn't matter
Latest is always the best"

"Oh, he has vertigo
Perhaps, the dope is yet to go
Off his system
Let us view his MRI
Don't forget to bill him for it"

"Urine negative, brain still good
The guy now doesn't urinate
Another tube will do him good
For the vertigo, dopes again
Good if he sleeps without pain"

The fever didn't subside
I was carted again
For procedures gastro-intestinal
As they wanted to see
What went on inside my entrails

So dopes again over dopes and dopes
"The guy doesn't complain
His entrails are clean
Now another issue
A lot he salivates
And aspirates, his lungs are inflamed"

"He has sores in the mouth
His gum bleeds
There are bed-sores
Groans and moans all the time
Looks like he is sinking
We have done everything
And his wallet has been drained"

"Let him go off supports
Parameters are good even though
Age perhaps is taking its toll
Isn't ninety a nice number to go"

"Give him palliative care
For the pain morphine
God will take further care
We will just wait, inform all who care"

So here I am, gasping for breath
God-forsaken, morphine helps
In daily increasing doses
Till such time my heart or breathing stops
Euthanasia of sorts
A word the world detests

When awareness rays in
Through desultory holes
On the roof of pitch darkness
How I long I was dying
A natural death in my village home

Coiled on a mat on the floor
Aches flowering on my brittle bones
Like a dog or cat, bird or rat
Watched by God from all the sides
As shadows play on uneven walls
A cuckoo sings a solitary song
Rain and sun play hide and seek
Refereed by the whistling wind

Oh God if thine other name
Is Consciousness, light those things
For a while, so I breathe my last in aches
With a smile flowering on my face

87. I Walked in the Drizzle

I took my morning stroll in the drizzle
Up and down in Tucson
An umbrella resting on my shoulder
Between a grandma mesquite
Hunchback, her trunk and branches
Badly lacerated through years and years
Of exploitation by inhuman humans
And a conifer pine
Thrusting his head into the empty sky
In deep meditation in a philosophical high

The mesquite was senile
Dilapidated infirm
Asthmatic in the rain
The pine a scholar
Base fulsome
Head tapering into the void

I walked my old age path

As the mountains looked down veiled

Like Arabian dames

Between the two

In that unceasing spray of rain

Reminiscing my teenage walks

Of miles and miles

In the drizzle

Just to spot a pair of eyes

Flash, mascara-lined

Behind a window curtain

Or watch a river in abandon

After night-long heavy rains

Teenage infatuations

They were

Sweet to reminisce

On this morn of incessant drizzle

An umbrella resting on my shoulder

Bones in sweet pain and languor

May I

Again look for those beautiful eyes

Behind a curtain

Or savour the fulsomeness

Of a youthful river in spate

Its course now bone-dry

88. The Ultimate Guru

(Written when Swami Dayananda Saraswati-ji entered samaadhi)

You entered my life like a blazing star
When I had my young head in the clouds
Inflated like a balloon
Thought the scriptures were my pocket diaries
Understood every word they spoke

You did my deflation silently
Without my knowledge
Made me know how little I knew
And then slowly
Imparted into me the knowing
That I am the whole; am everything

I didn't then realize
That you are the man
To whom I owed most in life
Till today when the news
Of your passing away
Welled my eyes
And drained my heart

You made me look at my body
Then at my thoughts
And then at the thinking me
The roles I played
Stages of life traversed
And asked me to remain
Ever the seeing me
Who is both being
And knowing too in one

You then made me dwell
On the fact that I am the self-shine
The worlds are made of to shine after
That I am the rose, I am the star
I am all that walked, flew and crawled
I am the rain, thunder, lightning
Everything that is a thing
Yet I am none but the fullest One
Eternal without a second
Beyond finitudinal counts and wants

You taught me
How to freely act
In the sea of actions
Without getting wet
On legitimate desires
And accept the fruits
Whatever they are
As gifts from the One above

You showed me the value of values
The value of acceptance
And surrender to the Universal Will
Till the mirror of the mind
Is cleaned to reflect
The pristine glory of the Self
As that same Supreme Will
Indwelling in everything

You took from me
The fear of change and death
They say you passed away
On the banks of the Ganges
The Sun of the morrow I am sure
Will miss a grey beard and smile
Yet you have no death, you live on
In me and the things I see
The Sun, Moon and the humming bird

The grieving mind grieves
In the ignorance of a loss that can't be
May Ma Ganges nurse you in her folds
And sing your eternal glory
As she traverses lands far and wide
That are accustomed to hearing
The universal songs of Truth
From our immemorial past

Soaked in prayerful tears I am
Oh Lord, bless us the ignorant bereaved
Peace, Peace, Peace!

89. The Cello That Played Tragic Notes

He sat on a granite stone
In the plantain grove
Motionless, unaware
Of the passage of time
Shadows lengthened
And shrank around

He was just about eight
Enamored by a tiny sunbird
Endeavoring at her nest
At the tip of a branch
That hung over the bamboo fence

A vigilant mate helped her
Together they brought
Material for the nest
Feathers, twigs, leaves, cotton wisps
Singing in joy as they passed

He sat like an idol
Unmindful of hunger
Thirst, numbness of limbs
Lest the birds were disturbed
If he moved or even batted his lashes

His parents had to drag him home
For lunch and breakfast
He would rush back to the stone
Gulping just a few mouthfuls
The nest had him swallowed full

The birds finished their build
Their home was done
The boy sat enchanted
Marveling at the avian abode

He couldn't suppress his joy
With his friends he shared
The secret of his glee
Pointing at the nest
Swaying in the wind
With the lady-bird perched on it
Her long beak busy
Finishing final details

Early next morn
He hurried to the grove
Without even pausing to brush his teeth
His heart broke
The nest was there no more

His friends had slashed the branch
The dream-house of the birds lay
On the ground infested by ants
Beside it was an unbroken egg
Dotted purple all over the shell

The boy broke down in anguish
His cheeks ran down flooded streams
Sat sobbing waiting
For the parent birds to descend
And save their tiny woebegone

It was soon noon and hot
He heard the birds wail aloft
But alas none ventured
Down to nurse the egg on the ground

He picked that hapless egg
Placed it on the red velvet
Of his mom's old jewel casket
Hoping one day it would hatch
A baby bird would emerge
And coo in a joy upsurge

Days and weeks passed
His dreams shriveled
As the egg dried and shrank
Broke open to expose
Remnants of an unsung song

The boy grew up to be a man
Who carried an unhatched egg
Of pain and song deep in the velvet
Of his bleeding heart
Wandered the world and wept
At wars, calamities, strifes
Wherever humanity stank

Perhaps he was born in an airy sign
Homed by a tearful moon
To carry a throbbing avian heart
Life-long like a high-strung cello
That played only tragic notes
Wail of unborn embryos
Stranded human souls

90. Waheeda Look-Alike

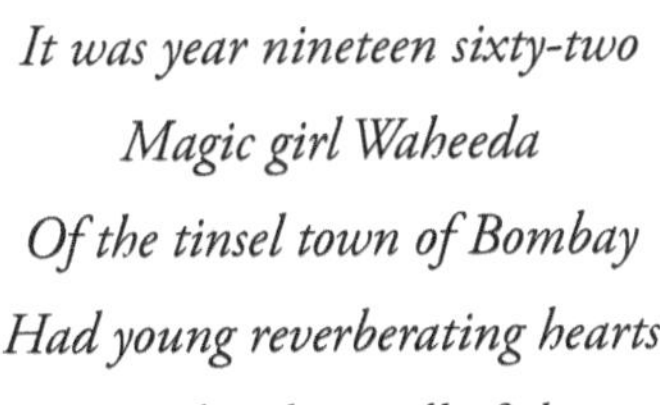

It was year nineteen sixty-two
Magic girl Waheeda
Of the tinsel town of Bombay
Had young reverberating hearts
Captured in her spell of charms

The haunting melody
"A lamp burnt somewhere
Somewhere a heart"
Flowed everywhere in the air
Monsoon wet
Filled with mist

I was just into college
When her look-alike arrived
In our midst
Same hairdo, veiled
Yet its front-line deliberately unveiled
To let a wisp of lock droop on a wide forehead
Eyes naughty, lovably cocky
Nose chiseled, sharp countenance

A total clone
That had me fallen
Head over heels
In a well of deep infatuation
And burning adoration
"A lamp burnt somewhere
Somewhere a heart"

I stood transfixed
As she passed
In and out of the college gate
Head bent, yet with a budding smile
That said she knew
Everything happening around

Soon it became a ritual
For me to wait at the gate
Motionless like a pillar
To see her pass by
Day after day
Without respite

So much so that
I became a part
Of the pompous gate
No one could any more
Tell me apart from it

She knew my presence
I was doubtless
How could my dogged devotion
Miss her attention? !
Yet never I could muster
Courage enough
To unbecome the pillar
And utter my heart

My silent worship
Consumed half a decade
Rains came, seasons changed
And every day she passed by
With that same budding smile
Watched by me, the worshipful pile

And on the last day
She looked directly into my eyes
Then bent her head again
Cupping her mouth
To suppress a laugh
And lo! I found her drop
A piece of paper on her path

As I ran with the winds
To capture the note
I saw her vanish from sight
In a darting haste across the street

That was the last
I ever saw of her
Perhaps, she got into wedded life
Hid in a burqa, mothered several kids
Sprayed attar day and night
Humming to motionless pillars in life
"A lamp burnt somewhere
Somewhere a heart"

And don't you want to know
What her final note had said?
"Be bold, ye stupid, adieu! "
Me the eternal pile placed at a gate

91. Unknown Pain

Why does twilight

Instill in me

A sadness?

Why does a lonely star

Make me go lachrymose?

Am not separated from a beloved

To empathize with a tearful moon

At age sixty nine

Yet, what is it that tears at my heart

An ache, is that existential?

God knows –

Yet, an unknown pain

Is that we carry

From birth till death

Like unwilling pall bearers

If that weren't the case
Of what avail is fancy
Depth of the night sky
Chirp of the lone sparrow
At nightfall
On the mountainside
Of what avail is poetry
At a pedestrian countryside?

Beautiful is pain
Am no masochist
Pain has poesy
As do sunsets
And the smiling Sirius
On a winter eve

Pain, pain and pain
Men tried to sink it in drinks
Here I remain
Eternally intoxicated
To weave the yarns
Of ceaseless poesy
Words please gather
Around my aching pen
So the pain of an unknown sunset
I can immortalize

92. Gaza

Someone posted
burning images of Gaza
subjected to relentless bombing.

He asked the world
"Did you sleep well?"

Yes, I slept well,
but that thought hurts,
am no hypocrite.

Let us not debate
how it all began;
that takes us nowhere
but only to more heat and hate.

We are all so accustomed
to blood, chaos and conflagration
and we do sleep,
peacefully so,
if all that is away from our door.

Some philosopher mused,
of the East he is for sure,
the world resides in you;
the pain you see
and moves you to trauma
is your inherent karma;
cleanse yourself therefore
if you are
to earn a cleaner world
than the one before your eyes.

We don't pause to think
but get out on the roads,
ask for justice.
Alas, there is no one there
to grant us what we want;
Gaza burns without respite.

To prayers therefore
I surrender.
Prayers, prayers and prayers,
perhaps, when I reopen my eyes
the world might smile,
no more blood smears,
bombing fires
and a looming apocalypse.
God bless us all,
whether He is named
Allah or the Lord;
He is there in all of us
shining without a pause,

93. Ganesh Chaturthi

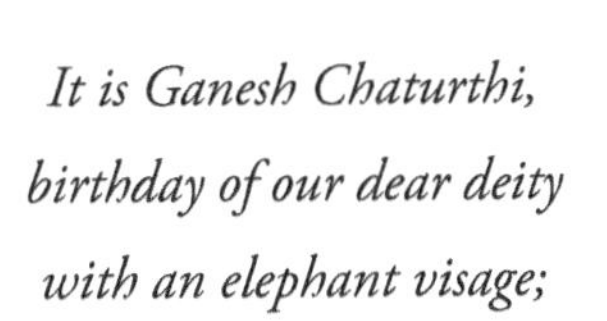

It is Ganesh Chaturthi,
birthday of our dear deity
with an elephant visage;
hymns and chants everywhere,
joyous crowds in cheer.

Elephants caparisoned,
besmirched with vermilion,
holy ashes, sandal paste,
are taken around on the streets
with drumbeats.
devotees piously prostrate.

The celebrations this year
have more heat and gusto,
for an atheist politician just two months ago
had dubbed the elephant God a myth
drawing tonnes of acid flak
from ardent detractors around the globe.

He was indeed wrong,
the deity can't be a myth,
when He is an inspiring presence
living and omnipresent in the hearts
of His devotees all over the earth
guiding them in their myriad paths.

But the tragedy — behold the mammoths
on the streets
surrounded by cheering crowds -
their legs are chained both back and front!

Chain, chain all over,
selfish to the core,
we like to keep the granter
of liberation from worldly woes,
the elephant God, our dear deity,
sadly bound and shackled in us.

Unchain Him, friends, and let us celebrate
In sheer, true abandon
His glorious birthday morn.

94. Aliens

At a gathering of UFO enthusiasts
in distant Mexico
boasting of an ancient past,
they displayed, it is said,
three cadavers preserved
of aliens who perished
several centuries ago.

They had only three fingers
on each hand,
unlike humans who have five;
that made the story credible.

Yet, why all this hullabaloo?
After all, they were no better
than us humans,
for both perish,
every second sadly change
till the final erasure by time.

Aliens are like us,
nothing at all outlandish!
Let us return
to our mundane worries
and win illusory accolades.

95. Rishi Sunak

Congrats!

You are Prime Minister of an Empire
on which the Sun has chosen to set.

I don't share the pride of many
who fondly believe that India has won
through your election
because you happen to share
their faith and common heritage.

Your forefathers were from my subcontinent - yes
you share the faith I was born in - yes
and you swore by its holy book - yes,
but that doesn't impress.

Impress us now
by proving your mettle,
bring back the sunken Sun
from down the waters of time
and make it shine again
over England,
lift her from the economic morass
she has sunk in.
A la Wordsworth mourned to Milton
"she is a fen of stagnant waters"
price-rise, chaos and Brexit.

Raise her up and give her pride,
heal her woes and give her back
that inner happiness she has lost

You have it in you, Sir
because you are versatile
in running a personal empire
of big fortune,
you are young and strong
with time on your side.

Do it Prime Minister
and then I will raise
a glass of sparkling cheers
to salute you and say
"See he has done it,
we share his genes"

96. Sardar

Patel, the steelman, India's own Sardar,
who tamed several quarrelsome, cacophonous
country states into a union – a songful garland!

How much we wish the whole of Kashmir
were in your grip like Hyderabad!
You could have re-written Indian history,
obviated the rivers of blood that flowed,
lives lost, the continuing conflict and misery.

That dream was not to flower -
Kashmir remained burning - a painful wound
on Mother India, causing streams of blood to flow
leaving you on your deathbed with an anguished heart
broken by the Mahatma's tragic exit.
Time then robbed you of us -
orphaned India drowned in tears.

Dreams still flower in vain-
had you been at the helm alone
of our freedom struggle,
perhaps, India would have remained undivided
and the Father of the Nation continued his triumph
on the path of non-violence.

You captained the Quit India Movement,
united our farmers and brought their brotherhood
into the cause of our freedom struggle.
Efficient and alacritous,
you proved a great Indian sage of action!

To you, her heroic son,
India today has dedicated
a statue of steel
over six hundred feet tall
on the banks of the peaceful Narmada,
Oh, you, the valorous son of Nadiad,
unparalleled architect of India!

Towering into the skies of blueness
in our hearts, you stand,
the great son of India,
whatever untruths your detractors,
the vested interests mouth.
Triumphant always, you our Sardar remain!

May India awake listening to your stories of valour!
May again Sardars descend on this land of the Ganges!
May they recapture the losses of the past!
May India continue eternally undivided!
May the Shambhu of Somnath, our guardian, protect!

97. The Peaceful Pacific

A road trip through the Pacific West,
from Seattle along Sequim,
Ocean Shore, Seaside,
all the way to San Francisco.
The Pacific roared beside.

Frequent signs warned of Tsunami hazard
While a warning at a trinket shop
showed an evacuation route,
an ice cream ad promised a tsunami of delight.

People thronged the beaches en route,
least worried, all in mirth;
a gigantic tide was last on their list.

At Ocean Shore, a man and woman
stood in tight embrace,
the lady sobbing without respite,
a personal tsunami on the heave,
wreaking havoc on their aching psyche.
The Pacific just looked on beside.

Humanity seemed a cluster of ants
on the rim of a tea-cup left under a tap
savouring their last greedy grabs,
weeping over what is not.
The tap looks down upon.

Yet, away, unknown to them
two superpowers were locked
in an eye-ball confrontation
over things of least real concern
portending a nuclear conflagration.

Lo, the Pacific stands for peace
as her name really means,
while men portend real nemesis,
their own apocalypse.

98. Love the Cow

*Yesterday, we were at Tillamook Creamery**
Where cheese-making was on display
Love the cows and treat them like queens
There were messages umpteen
I was thrilled the West too thought Indian

We roamed viewing different processes
Of making a variety of cheese
Till the products are packed nice at the end
To reach households worldwide
And make every consumer content

After tasting their free samples
And an ice cream delicious
The question popped into my mind
What happens to our much-loved friends
When they go dry at the end?

Pat came the reply: "We love Beef"
Where is the reason for disbelief?!

**Tillamook Creamery, Oregon, USA, manufactures a variety of milk products and markets them worldwide. They have a fantastic display centre.*

99. Ode to Sandy

Sandy

Superstorm Sandy

You are a blessing

To sensational journalism

And reporting

For those who indulge

In prophesies

Of wanton apocalypse

The likes of you

Have had several landfalls

On Mother Earth

Even before

And yet at any time

One of you ransacks

Our comforts and pleasures

We come out of our homes

Hold a microphone

And cry out aloud

The end of the world is around

And here I sit
Looking at an overcast sky
Half-naked in heat
Somewhere in the south
Of the vast Indian subcontinent
Where the mountains still breathe
Sultry warmth in passionate fervor
At a time the North East should pour
Her bounteous benedictions
Alas! Only barren clouds overhead
Unlikely to deliver
A much needed shower

Sandy
Why don't you cast
Your looks this way
So that our kids on the streets
Naked to their hilt
Dance in a deluge
And forget the fire
In their stomach
At least for once?

We don't care much
Accustomed to wraths
Of Mother Nature
No one here holds
A microphone
To lament our deaths

Sandy,
Am I asking for too much?
Won't you just look our way
And shun the TV gibberish
To embrace us, the impoverished?

(With profuse apologies to those who have suffered at the hands of Sandy)

100. Nightingales Don't Die

I never had an ear for music,
my design always shuddered at lyrics;
that is the way I am made,
my ears and vocal chords fail to resonate.

I have walked the dusty streets
in the bustle of our cities,
both small and big,
and the unpopulated wilderness,
watched sunset and sunrise
from mountain tops, deserts and sea-sides.

And wherever I went
a nightingale always crooned.
Didn't bother who that was
or where she hid,
for something in me melted in that melody,
though unknown were its subtle metrics,
frequency, waves,
or the tongue whether it was
Hindi, Marathi, some other language.

And now people say
the nightingale has flown away
into the folds of time;
how can that be?

The croon I hear here,
there, everywhere,
it can't leave me
but only fill my inside
with nectar even when I lie
dead on a mountainside
listening to a songful passerine.

For nightingales don't die
and me too with Lata-ji
the nightingale inside me,
crooning, crooning and crooning.